NEW DIRECTIONS FOR ADULT AND CONTINUING EDUCATION

Susan Imel, *Ohio State University*
EDITOR-IN-CHIEF

D0902711

Promoting Journal Writing in Adult Education

Leona M. English
Saint Francis Xavier University

Marie A. Gillen
Saint Francis Xavier University

EDITORS

Number 90, Summer 2001

JOSSEY-BASS
San Francisco

PROMOTING JOURNAL WRITING IN ADULT EDUCATION
Leona M. English, Marie A. Gillen (eds.)
New Directions for Adult and Continuing Education, no. 90
Susan Imel, Editor-in-Chief

Microfilm copies of issues and articles are available in 16mm and 35mm, as well as microfiche in 105mm, through University Microfilms Inc., 300 North Zeeb Road, Ann Arbor, Michigan 48106-1346.

ISSN 1052-2891   ISBN 0-7879-5774-7

NEW DIRECTIONS FOR ADULT AND CONTINUING EDUCATION is part of The Jossey-Bass Higher and Adult Education Series and is published quarterly by Jossey-Bass, 350 Sansome Street, San Francisco, California 94104-1342.

SUBSCRIPTIONS cost $59.00 for individuals and $114.00 for institutions, agencies, and libraries.

EDITORIAL CORRESPONDENCE should be sent to the Editor-in-Chief, Susan Imel, ERIC/ACVE, 1900 Kenny Road, Columbus, Ohio 43210-1090. E-mail: imel.1@osu.edu.

Cover photograph by Wernher Krutein/PHOTOVAULT © 1990.

www.josseybass.com

CONTENTS

Editors' Notes

"Writing bridges the inner and outer worlds and connects the paths of action and reflection" (Baldwin, 1991, p. 9). These words are a partial answer to the questions: What is so special about journal writing? Why is journal writing such a powerful vehicle for fostering adult learning? The answer is simple: journal writing provides those occasions that can help one "to find out what's in your heart and at the bottom of your mind" (Bender, 1999, p. 1). Journal writing fosters personal and professional learning. It is a way to break out of the defensive cover that protects us from the offensive realities of social, political, and cultural everyday living. These realities, unless addressed, can become barriers to learning. Journal writing is one way to overcome these barriers because it provides a means of self-expression, a way of stirring oneself to sensibility—that is, fostering the capacity to respond to intellectual, emotional, and aesthetic stimuli.

What is journal writing? How is its purpose defined? In response to these questions, a brief review of the literature provides some answers from different perspectives. For example, Apps (1994) refers to journal writing as "a valuing process" (p. 197) because it helps one to sort out what is really important. Similarly, Wlodkowski (1999) describes journal writing as "an informative complement to more conventional forms of assessment" (p. 268). It is a vehicle that can help adult learners answer questions like these: How do I know that I know? What is the evidence? Why is this information important? How will I use this information? McAlpine (1992) takes a different view. She refers to journals as "professional conversations" during which "we can write a description of the things that happened . . . relive our feelings and emotions associated with the events . . . reflect on the feelings and events in order to relate this experience to others" (p. 15). O'Hanlon (1997) refers to journals as a basis for self-reflection. She identifies four spontaneous modes of journal practice: report writing, interpretive writing, deliberative writing, and integrative writing; each refers to "thinking and reflection which range from a mere description of educational events to a more profound self-aware and evaluative mode" (p. 173). In her discussion of journal writing, Bender (1999) uses the metaphor of fertile ground. She describes journal writing as an abundantly productive way of learning, because it is a continuing activity that provides a link joining the past, present, and future. In other words, journal writing has a productive influence because it encourages the writer to look at things from both a retrospective and prospective point of view. These ideas relating to journal writing echo the views of many other adult educators, including us.

This brief review of the literature shows that journals are recommended as a way for adult learners to reflect on action and practice; nevertheless, little is written on the overall benefits of journal writing, how journals are to be integrated into learning and assessment, and what the ethical concerns of using journals are. The general lack of investigation into the use of journals signals, yet once again, adult educators' unquestioning acceptance of educational trends, without a critical analysis of how they can be used to foster learning.

In this volume, we define journal writing as an art and a science. As an art, a journal is a product or expression of what is more than ordinary experience; it is a creative and imaginative way of describing one's thoughts, feelings, and actions. As a science, a journal helps the writer to engage in reflection intentionally and systematically. We find metaphors a good way to describe journal writing as a learning technique. It can be compared to the formation of a beautiful rainbow. This comparison is appropriate because some of the most beautiful rainbows in the world, at least in our view, can be seen in Antigonish, Nova Scotia, where our university is located. A basic ingredient of both processes, the formation of a rainbow and the writing of a learning journal, is internal reflection. The kind of reflection the rainbow requires is defined by the laws of physics; the kind required for a learning journal is defined by learning theory. These differences aside, internal reflection is an important ingredient of both processes. Both processes also rely on illumination by a strong light: the rainbow with illumination by the sun and the learning journal with illumination by the human mind. A rainbow is described as a set of colored arcs seen against the sky, whereas a journal is a tapestry of events seen against a backdrop of human life. Both are pleasing, authentic, and good.

In our view, adult learners need to think deeply about their personal and professional experiences. We have found that one effective way for doing this is journal writing. A cornerstone of our program, a self-directed master of adult education program that has a professional development focus, is reflective practice. As a way to foster this practice, we incorporate journal writing into the learning experience in order to facilitate an understanding of self in a professional context. As part of the process of introducing this strategy, we inquire as to whether our students have used journals previously and for what purpose. The experiences they identify are quite diverse: recording workplace events, taking field notes as part of an action research project, enhancing personal or professional development, and documenting readings for academic purposes.

Although there is potential for growth and learning through journal writing, not all students enjoy the task. When we start to discuss journal writing with our students, it is not unusual that negative comments surface: "Not again!" "Why do we have to do a journal?" "Can't it be an optional requirement?" The less enthusiastic students often need to be convinced of the value of journal writing, and they need guidance. Apps (1994) points out the many ways that journal writing is beneficial. Some of these benefits—for example, discovering what I know that I am not aware of knowing, creating new ideas, sorting out what is important, or creating a permanent record—often convince reluctant students that journal writing deserves a serious try. Wlodkowski (1999) advises students who need guidance "to pay less attention to the mechanics and organization and to whether or not their writing makes sense"; he encourages them to "simply try to get their thoughts and feelings down on paper where they can learn from them" (p. 269). Some authors who have contributed chapters to this volume provide other suggestions of how students, especially the wry and timid, can be gently guided through the journal writing process.

We discovered in our review of the literature two areas of adult education that routinely integrate journal writing into practice: literacy education (Palmer, Alexander, and Olson-Dinges, 1999) and English as a Second Language (ESL) (Orem, 1997). The literature is replete with examples of how those who work as literacy instructors use journals with their students as a way to increase reflection and learning. Interestingly, Kerka (1996), who has made one of the few attempts to bring an adult education framework to journals, draws on these two areas to make her point. However, few empirical studies and little theoretical literature relating to the use of journals in adult education are available (Holt, 1994). Faced with this paucity, we recognized the need for a sourcebook that provides a rationale and builds a basis for the use of journal writing in adult education and that promotes journal writing as a bona-fide strategy for fostering adult learning.

The chapters in this volume explore how adult educators integrate journal writing into the learning process in a variety of educational contexts: health education, the education of women, ESL, and higher education. We invite you to examine your own practice in the light of these chapters and ask yourself the following questions: Is journal writing a requirement in the courses I teach? If the answer is yes, ask, How do I integrate it into my courses? Is journal writing an optional component? If so, what purpose does it serve? What kind of guidance do I offer students when I require them to keep a journal? How do I use journal writing as a learning technique? We hope that the following chapters, written by adult educators who have incorporated journal writing into their courses, will help you to reflect on your practice and will provide answers to these questions.

The first four chapters set the stage for the development of the practical uses of journals in a variety of settings in the four chapters that follow. The final chapter summarizes the various chapters and raises issues for practitioners to consider.

David Boud, in Chapter One, points out that journal writing is used for many different purposes, but his focus is the use of journal writing as a way to enhance reflective practice. He explains the models of reflection and then explicates the occasions of reflection, such as reflection in anticipation of events, reflection in the midst of action, and reflection after events. He then focuses on features of journal writing that can inhibit reflection, such as the questioning of taken-for-granted assumptions about oneself, the prospect that others will read the journal, and the fact that someone will grade and assess the journal. Boud concludes that the conditions under which journals are written can influence what is produced and, more important, the extent to which the adult learner can engage in critical reflection.

Roger Hiemstra's ideas, set out in Chapter Two, focus on the uses and benefits of journal writing as an instructional or learning tool in adult education. He describes types and formats for journal writing, including learning journals; diaries; dream books or logs; autobiographies, life stories, and memoirs; spiritual journals; professional journals; interactive reading logs; theory logs; and electronic journaling, which can be used with any of the types and formats for journal writing already listed. Among the potential benefits of journal writing that he identifies are personal growth and development, self-discovery, problem solving, stress reduction and health benefits, and the ability to reflect critically. The chapter ends with some suggestions for overcoming obstacles to journal writing and a recommendation that adult educators and their students try one of the techniques that he has described.

In Chapter Three, Leona English centers attention on ethical concerns relating to journal writing and cautions that ethical questions should not be trivialized. She focuses on the ethical issues that arise from journal writing, such as the intersection of the personal and the professional and how journal entries will be assessed. To make her point, she provides five ethical problems based on adult education practice—but she does not provide answers. Rather, she presents readers with several queries to ponder relating specifically to each case. English ends the chapter with a set of principles that adult educators who use journal writing in their practice can refer to when faced with ethical questions. In her view, the ultimate ethical question is whether we are committed to our own ethical practice, to evaluating our own learning, and to living out of the questions that arise out of our practice.

Tara Fenwick begins Chapter Four with personal recollections of using journal writing in her professional practice and then focuses on the nature of the responsive relationship. She discusses different modes of response, issues of confession and power when responding to journals, and the need to balance direction and freedom in assisting the journal writer. She offers many suggestion for how adult educators can respond to someone's journal writing by using what she refers to as respectful dialogue. Fenwick offers criteria that are often used to assess journal writing and provides a sample rating scale for evaluating journals. She cautions adult educators to be absolutely clear about their purpose and rationale for responding to journals, as well as their potentially repressive influence on the journal writer.

The subject of Chapter Five, by Angela Gillis, is the use of journals in nursing education, as well as their role in continuing professional education for nurses and other health professionals working in clinical settings. She defines a journal in the health education context as a process and a product. In her view, journals are useful in locating the personal in the fast-paced health care environments that are increasingly dominated by technology and impersonal procedures. She describes a three-step method of journal writing that has proven useful at the university where she teaches in preparing graduates who are capable of critical analysis, self-reflection, self-evaluation, enhanced self-awareness, and self-directed learning. She also sets out practical guidelines for writing journal entries, suggestions for how journal writing can be used as a tool for learning in continuing competence programs, and implications of and future trends regarding the use of journals in health education settings.

Elizabeth Peterson and Ann Jones explain in Chapter Six how journal writing plays an important role in women's lives by helping them to regain their voices. They explore the various ways that women use journals and how this technique aids the reflective process. They highlight three kinds of barriers to journal writing that women often face: attitudinal, situational, and dispositional. They provide several examples of women's journal writing that support their belief that journals suit women's ways of knowing very well. The chapter contains suggestions on how women can be encouraged to use journal writing to speak in their own voice, listen to their internal voice, and change their meaning perspectives. They conclude that journals are a source of encouragement and hope for the women who write them and for those who read them.

In Chapter Seven, Richard Orem elaborates on the use of journals in ESL classes and as a way of improving practice through reflective writing. He discusses the role of journal writing as a technique in the preparation and continuing education of ESL teachers, as well as a teaching technique in adult ESL classrooms. During ESL teacher preparation, journal writing is used to record observations and responses to events that occur in the teaching-learning transaction. ESL teachers can also use journals as a way to deal with the isolation that many of them experience in their practice. Orem offers many suggestions on how this can be done. In his discussion of the role of journal writing as a teaching technique, he explores how the use of journals depends on the approach to ESL that is being used. Throughout the chapter, he uses many examples to make his points. For both ESL teachers and students, journal writing provides the vehicle for reflection that leads to more effective practice.

In Chapter Eight, Peter Jarvis laments the paucity of literature on the use of journal writing in higher education. Consequently, much of what he presents is drawn from his own professional experience. His chapter examines the use of journals in undergraduate and postgraduate education, the personal use of journals in postgraduate distance teaching, and the use of journals in research. He draws on the literature for examples and refers to two uses of learning journals with which he has been involved: distance and mixed-mode delivery professional education. He also describes how some of his doctoral students have been using journals in a variety of research settings. He concludes that learning journals are an invaluable tool that should be practiced and taught much more widely in higher education circles.

In the last chapter, we discuss the reasons that make the integration of a journal writing component into adult education so difficult, such as a lack of practice-related knowledge and institutional forces that block such initiatives, or co-opt these to serve their own selfish ends. We also identify resources that can be used to assist adult educators in using journals in their practice.

This volume of *New Directions for Adult and Continuing Education* is truly a collective effort, and we are indebted to everyone who helped us to bring our dream of this volume to reality, especially those who so generously volunteered to contribute a chapter when we asked. The authors represent four countries (Australia, Canada, England, and the United States), quite a feat for a volume of this size. We also acknowledge the financial support of the University Council for Research at Saint Francis Xavier University in completing this work.

We are more convinced now than we were before we began to work on this volume of the potential for personal growth and learning through journal writing. It can be used to help people to reflect on their learning and experiences in such a way that they develop a clearer sense of themselves as practitioners and as individuals who have the personal means to improve and grow in their profession. The words of Martin Buber (1948) are particularly appropriate here: "Each of us is encased in an armour which we soon, out of familiarity, cease to notice. There are only moments which penetrate it and stir the soul to sensibility" (p. 10). Journal writing provides those moments for everyone who engages in this process.

Leona M. English
Marie A. Gillen

References

Apps, J. W. *Leadership for the Emerging Age: Transforming Practice and Continuing Education.* San Francisco: Jossey-Bass, 1994.

Baldwin, C. *Life's Companion: Journal Writing as a Spiritual Quest.* New York: Bantam Books, 1991.

Bender, S. "Thirteen Steps to Stronger Journal Writing." *Writers Digest,* 1999, 79, 18–19.

Buber, M. *Between Man and Man.* (R. G. Smith, trans.). New York: Macmillan, 1948.

Holt, S. *Reflective Journal Writing and Its Effects in Adults.* Columbus, Ohio: ERIC Clearinghouse on Adult, Career, and Vocational Education, 1994. (ED 375 302)

Kerka, S. *Journal Writing and Adult Learning.* Columbus, Ohio: Clearinghouse on Adult, Career, and Vocational Education, 1996. (ED 399 416). [www.ericacue.org/docs/dig174.htm]

McAlpine, L. "Learning to Reflect: Journals as Professional Conversations." *Adult Learning,* 1992, 3, 15, 23, 24.

O'Hanlon, C. "The Professional Journal: Journals as Professional Conversations." In S. Hollingsworth (ed.), *International Action Research: A Casebook for Educational Reform.* Bristol, Pa.: Falmer Press, 1997.

Orem, R. A. "Journal Writing as a Form of Professional Development." Paper presented at the Midwest Research-to-Practice Conference in Adult, Continuing, and Community Education, 1997.

Palmer, B. C., Alexander, M.M.C., and Olson-Dinges, C. "Journal Writing: An Effective Heuristic Method for Literacy Acquisition." *Adult Basic Education*, 1999, 9, 71–89.

Wlodkowski, R. J. *Enhancing Motivation to Learn.* (Rev. ed.). San Francisco: Jossey-Bass, 1999.

Leona M. English is associate professor of adult education at Saint Francis Xavier University, Antigonish, Nova Scotia.

Marie A. Gillen is professor of adult education at Saint Francis Xavier University, Antigonish, Nova Scotia.

1

Journals promote reflection on experience. This chapter examines features of journal writing that aid reflective practice and circumstances inhibiting their use for this purpose.

Using Journal Writing to Enhance Reflective Practice

David Boud

Adult educators write journals for many different reasons prompted by many different purposes. We may want to capture an experience, record an event, explore our feelings, or make sense of what we know. We may want to narrate something of importance so that others can see what we saw in it. Sometimes we write primarily for ourselves, sometimes for others. Journal writing is as varied as those who engage in it.

Journal writing can be viewed through many different lenses: as a form of self-expression, a record of events, or a form of therapy. It can be a combination of these and other purposes. In this chapter, I examine journal writing through the lens of learning. I present it as a form of reflective practice, that is, as a device for working with events and experiences in order to extract meaning from them. This perspective views the various forms of journal writing as ways of making sense of the world and how we operate within it. Journal writing can be used to enhance what we do and how we do it. As a vehicle for learning, it can be used in formal courses, our professional practice, or any aspect of informal learning.

In her discussion of using journals in learning through reflection, Moon (1999a, pp. 188–194) identifies many purposes of writing journals in addition to those already mentioned—for example:

"To deepen the quality of learning, in the form of critical thinking or developing a questioning attitude"
"To enable learners to understand their own learning process"
"To increase active involvement in learning and personal ownership of learning"

NEW DIRECTIONS FOR ADULT AND CONTINUING EDUCATION, no. 90, Summer 2001
© John Wiley & Sons, Inc.

"To enhance professional practice or the professional self in practice"
"To enhance the personal valuing of the self towards self-empowerment"
"To enhance creativity by making better use of intuitive understanding"
"To free-up writing and the representation of learning"
"To provide an alternative `voice' for those not good at expressing themselves"
"To foster reflective and creative interaction in a group"

Learning is inherent in any process of expression, that is, in any way of giving form to the world as experienced. No matter what the reason is for which we write, the lens of learning is an important way of viewing writing. This is not to say that learning is the only perspective on journal writing, but rather to acknowledge that journal writing is intimately associated with learning, no matter what else it may aim to do.

Learning and Reflection

There are many ways of thinking about journal writing in relation to learning. We can look at how journals reveal what their writers have learned, examine how writers have learned to express themselves in journals, or find out how journals can help other people to learn. The most important purpose for this chapter is how individuals can use journals to enhance their own learning.

The process of exploring how journals can assist their writers to learn is commonly described in terms of how journals can enhance reflection and reflective practice. Reflection has been described as a process of turning experience into learning, that is, a way of exploring experience in order to learn new things from it. Boud, Keogh, and Walker (1985) have described reflection as "those intellectual and affective activities in which individuals engage to explore their experiences in order to lead to new understandings and appreciations" (p. 19).

Reflection involves taking the unprocessed, raw material of experience and engaging with it as a way to make sense of what has occurred. It involves exploring often messy and confused events and focusing on the thoughts and emotions that accompany them. Reflection can be undertaken as an informal personal activity for its own sake or as a part of a structured course. Within a course, reflection may focus on special activities (for example, workshop activities), events of the past (for example, what learners bring to the course from prior experience), or concurrent activities in the learners' workplace and community that act as a stimulus for learning. In this chapter, the word *event* is used to refer to any activity from which learning may result, whether it happens in a classroom, a workshop, a formally scheduled placement, or everyday life.

Any of these events provides the base material for journal writing and reflective practice. In learning terms, the journal is both the place where the events and experiences are recorded and the forum by which they are processed and re-formed. This working with events is intended as a way to make sense of the experiences that result, recognize the learning that results, and build a foundation for new experiences that will provoke new learning.

Models of Reflection

The most familiar approach to reflection was developed by the late Donald Schön in his books on the reflective practitioner (1983, 1987). Schön argues that a vital attribute of all effective practitioners, no matter in what area they operate, is that they are able to reflect on their ongoing experience and learn from it. He describes examples of architects, musicians, therapists, teachers, and others, all reflecting on what they do as they go about their everyday practice. He calls this approach *reflection-in-action*. Just as important as this approach, however, is the considered reflection that takes place away from the press of immediate action when we pause and take stock of what we are doing. This type of reflection may occur driving home at the end of the day, in the bathtub, or when discussing with colleagues or friends what we do.

It is in this second category that journal writing most often fits, because writing is a means of puzzling through what is happening in our work and our personal lives. In some courses, journal writing is formalized even further, and specific guidelines and workbooks may be provided. However, here I focus on the features of reflection that aid learning independent of particular course requirements. Later in the chapter, I discuss how some course requirements and the influences of the contexts in which journal writing takes place inadvertently inhibit the very learning that journal writing is designed to foster.

In parallel with Schön's work on reflective practice (1983, 1987), I have been involved in exploring reflection from the point of view of someone who is trying to learn from his normal complex and unruly experience. Over a number of years, I have been involved with colleagues in developing a model for learning from experience and the place of reflection in it. Our purpose has been to provide a means of focusing the attention of learners, and those who assist them, on some of the key features that either inhibit or facilitate learning (Boud, Keogh, and Walker, 1985; Boud and Walker, 1990, 1998). Each aspect of the model has implications for journal writing.

To highlight the varieties and forms of journal writing, which are discussed elsewhere in this book and can be used to facilitate reflection and learning from experience, I describe the main features of the model and discuss the implications for journal writing of each feature in turn.

The basic assumption of the model is that learning is always grounded in prior experience and that any attempt to promote new learning must take into account that experience. All learning builds on existing perceptions and frameworks of understanding; therefore, links must be made between what is new and what already exists if learners are to make sense of what is happening to them. Learners bring to any event their personal foundation of experience. This is a way of describing the influence of all their previous experiences on them now. Past experiences profoundly affect perceptions of what does and does not count as important; they act as a way to sensitize us to some features of our world and blind us to others, and they shape the intent we have that guides our priorities.

The second assumption is that the process of learning from experience is necessarily an active one, involving learners' engaging with the events of which they are part. Much of the benefit of participating in any event derives from how we can shape our participation to suit our goals.

Occasions of Reflection

Although reflection is conventionally thought of as taking place after something has happened, such a view depicts learners as passive respondents to events. To counteract this idea, it is useful to consider three occasions of reflection: in anticipation of events, during them, and afterward. Journal writing has a significant role to play at each of these times.

Reflection in Anticipation of Events. The emphasis here is on what we can do to make the most of future events. In other words, what might usefully be taken into account in preparing ourselves for what is to come? Although we can never predict fully what will occur, the model suggests that there are three main aspects to take into account. First is a focus on the learner. What intents and specific goals do we bring to the event? What are our expectations of the event and the outcomes? How strongly do we hold our intents, and will these blind us to other possibilities of which we are as yet unaware? Journals can be used to explore what we want from our involvement in any activity. We write about what we bring to the event, what we want out of it, and what we need to be mindful of that may distract us from our intentions. The more complex and unfamiliar the situation is, the more difficult it will be to keep track of the reasons for being there.

Second is a focus on all aspects of the context. Many, if not most, of the features of an event usually are given and cannot be altered. Sometimes we are briefed on what might happen, but often we have to discover these possibilities for ourselves. Journal writing helps to clarify questions we need to address about the event we are entering, that is, what we need to know to make the event a productive one for us. Other people may have quite different ideas about what will happen. This is particularly true of work placements, where the learner must fit with the everyday practices of the workplace. How do people there view things, and what are the implications for us? Journals can be used here to record what we know of the context and what is possible.

Third is a focus on learning skills and strategies. It is not sufficient to focus on what we bring to the context and what it will be like; we also need to equip ourselves to make use of the opportunities available. What must we notice in order to be fully involved and understand what is going on? What guides or learning-to-learn strategies can we usefully develop and take with us? What might we need to rehearse before we start? Journals allow us to practice imaginary scenarios; ask "What if?"; plan what we need to take to the event; try out forms of record keeping that might be suitable; and practice conversations and interactions with key players we will meet. Useful questions to ask at this stage are, What will I do if my assumptions about the event are wrong? What will I be able to fall back on in order to cope effectively?

Reflection in the Midst of Action. Our engagement with an event constitutes a learning experience. The model points to key features of learning in the midst of action. Through noticing, intervening, and reflection-in-action, we can steer ourselves through events in accordance with what our intentions are and with what we take with us to help us through the process.

Noticing. This feature is about becoming aware of what is happening in and around us. It is directed toward both the external world of events and the internal world of thoughts and feelings. Noticing affects the extent to which we become actively involved in the process, whether or not this fact is observable by others.

Intervening. This feature refers to actions we take to change the situation in which we find ourselves. Again, intervening may not be overt and noticeable to others. The conscious decision not to speak, or to focus attention on thoughts and feelings rather than external activities, are forms of intervention (intervention in our internal learning processes), just as much as a provocative question or a physical act.

Reflection-in-Action. This feature describes the process of all three features working together to interpret events and the effects of one's interventions. For much of the time, these features are invisible and unconscious, and as Schön (1983, 1987) eloquently points out, they are part of the artistry of effective practice. However, in developing expertise of any kind, it is often helpful to become more deliberate and conscious of the process and more aware of the decisions being made by others and ourselves. It is through exposing these decisions to scrutiny that the assumptions behind them can be identified and a conscious decision to act from a new perspective can be taken.

Although there may be few opportunities to write in the heat of the moment when events are rapidly changing, enough information needs to be recorded to prompt fuller exploration when there is time to do so. On some occasions, it may be possible to schedule time for reflection. This can be particularly useful in some work placements. Journal writing can be used to prompt an awareness of new features of the situation, plan new interventions that can be implemented almost immediately, and observe the effects.

Reflection After Events. Much important reflection can occur once the immediate pressure of acting in real time has passed. Some learning inevitably takes time and requires the ability to view particular events in a wider context. Reflection following events has been discussed in the literature for many years, but it is important to emphasize that it is not simply a process of thinking, but a process that also involves feelings, emotions, and decision making. We can regard it as having three elements: return to experience, attending to feelings, and reevaluation of experience. These are features of reflection at all stages, and what is written here is also applicable at earlier stages.

Return to Experience. The base of all learning is the lived experience of the learner. To return to this experience and recapture it in context with its full impact allows for further reflection. Often, too little emphasis is placed on what has happened and how it was experienced at the time. Judgments made in this way are often premature; consequently, possibilities for further learning can be shut out forever. Mentally revisiting and vividly portraying the experience in writing can be an important first step. The role of journal writing here is to give an account of what happened and to retrieve as fully as possible the rich texture of events as they unfolded. The emphasis is on conjuring up the situation afresh and capturing it in a form that enables it to be revisited with ease.

Attending to Feelings. As part of returning to the experience, we need to focus on the feelings and emotions that were (or are) present. These feelings can inhibit or enhance possibilities for further reflection and learning. Feelings experienced as negative may need to be discharged or sublimated; otherwise, they may continually distort all other perceptions and block understanding. Those experienced as positive can be celebrated, because they enhance the desire to pursue learning.

Expressive writing has a particular role to play in working with feelings. Journals are not just the place for writing prose. Images, sketches, poems, and the use of color and form are among devices that can be used as vehicles to express ways of experiencing. Stream-of-consciousness writing, in which words are poured out without pause for punctuation, spelling, or self-censorship, can be of value here. Rainer (1980) has many good examples of expressive forms of writing.

Reevaluation of Experience. Reacquaintance with the event and attending to and expressing the thoughts and feelings associated with it can prepare the ground for freer evaluation of experience than is often possible at the time. The process of reevaluation includes relating new information to that which is already known, seeking relationships between new and old ideas, determining the authenticity for ourselves of the ideas and feelings that have resulted, and making the resulting knowledge one's own, that is, a part of one's normal ways of operating. These aspects of reevaluation should not be thought of as stages through which learners should pass, but parts of a whole to be taken up as needed for any particular purpose.

These reflective processes can be undertaken in isolation from others, but doing so often leads to a reinforcement of existing views and perceptions. Working in pairs or with a group for which learning is reason for being can begin to transform perspectives and challenge old patterns of learning. It is only through a give and take with others and by confronting the challenges they pose that critical reflection can be promoted.

Reevaluation is about finding shape, pattern, and meaning in what has been produced. It involves revisiting journal entries, looking again at what has been recorded, and adding new ideas and extensions to those partially formed. It addresses the question: What sense can I make of this, and where does it lead me? It involves trying out new ideas and asking, "What if?" Reevaluation is the end of one cycle and the beginning of another as new situations are imagined and explored.

Inhibiting Reflection

So far, this chapter has focused on occasions of reflection and the ways that journal writing can be used at different times and in different modes. However, there are many features of the contexts in which writing occurs that get in the way of learning and block reflection completely. The exploration of the self that reflection involves requires a relatively protected environment in which one is not continually preoccupied by defending oneself from the scrutiny of others. This is not to say that journal writing cannot usefully take place in the most adverse of conditions. The prison diaries and notebooks of such thinkers as Dietrich Bonhoeffer (1997) and Antonio Gramsci (1971) give testimony to the power of reflective writing. The conditions of contemporary journal writers in formal courses may be less physically oppressive, but nonetheless they can inhibit reflection.

The more that journal writing moves into the realm of critical reflection, that is, the questioning of taken-for-granted assumptions about oneself, one's group, or the conditions in which one operates, the more it is necessary to consider the inhibiting gaze of others. The more that journals are used to focus on those characteristics of reflection such as perplexity, hesitation, doubt (Dewey, 1933), inner discomforts (Brookfield, 1987), or disorienting dilemmas (Mezirow and others, 1990), the greater the need is to take into account the interventions of those who may read one's writing.

Who Is the Reader? One of the main inhibitors is the prospect of others' reading one's journal. These could be peers, employers, teachers, or indeed anyone else. The expectation of writing for an external audience can profoundly shape what we write and even what we allow ourselves to consider. (Other chapters in this volume pick up on this point, especially Chapters Three and Four.) The range of consequences of having one's writing read by others can range from mild embarrassment to loss of a job, or even worse. For example, revealing negative feelings about the difficulties of classroom practice could have a substantial influence on how a student teacher is perceived by supervisors and may lead to failure to graduate. Whether this is the reality of the situation, simply imagining such an occurrence may be a barrier to recording such feelings.

Keeping journals private, away from the eyes of others, can be a useful principle to adopt in courses. It means that writing may not be as constrained as it would be if it were revealed to others. At the very least, the postponing of decisions about whether writing is to be revealed, to whom, and in what form can be liberating. It can release creativity and a flow of thoughts and feelings that can always be censored and shaped for others to read.

Formal Assessment. Many of the ideas about learning from experience have developed in situations unconstrained by the requirements of educational institutions. Therefore, great care needs to be taken in translating them into a formal setting. One feature of accredited learning has considerable potential to adversely affect learning through journal writing: the assessment practices of the program in which a student is enrolled. (Fenwick discusses this in Chapter Four.) A common example is that of grading and assessing journals.

The conventions of assessment demand that students display their best work for it to be judged. Students therefore are interested in portraying themselves in the best light possible. It is in their interest to demonstrate what they know and disguise what they do not know—an attitude that is quite the opposite of that required for reflection. Reflection involves a focus on uncertainty, perplexing events, and exploration without necessarily knowing where it will lead. It is in the interest of learning that writers express their doubts, reveal their lack of understanding, and focus on what they do not know. Consequently, there is a tension between assessment and reflection that must be addressed in all courses where it may arise.

In my own teaching, I encourage students to keep portfolios of reflective material but inform them from the start that these do not have to be submitted to me. I point out that unless they feel sufficiently free to write things in their journals that they would be embarrassed for me to read, then they are probably not using their journals sufficiently well for them to be good examples of reflection. This does not mean that students cannot use items from their journals in their assignments, but they understand the clear separation of writing for learning and writing for assessment purposes. In order to emphasize this distinction, I include as one assignment the production of a self-assessment statement that draws from, but is distinct from, students' confidential learning portfolios (Boud, 1992).

In some situations, it may be appropriate to assess journals (Moon 1999b; see also Chapters Three and Four in this volume). These include preparation for professional practice in which the use of case notes and commentaries on them is part of normal work. However, it is important to distinguish from the start journals that are essentially available for public or semipublic inspection and those designed to prompt reflection. It is misleading to treat all forms of journal writing as equivalent to each other. Their purposes constrain their form, and the use of a single term like *journal writing* to convey such widely differing purposes is confusing and risky.

Conclusion

Journal writing is a multifaceted activity that can take many forms for many purposes. It can be used in many different ways to promote reflection. Different strategies and devices can be used at different stages of learning to focus on events anticipated, as well as those that have passed.

The conditions under which journal writing takes place can have a powerful influence on what is produced and the extent to which writers can engage in critical reflection. If journals are to be used in courses, great care needs to be taken about how they relate to assessed work. In general, reflective activities should be distinguished from those graded.

References

Bonhoeffer, D. *Letters and Paper from Prison*. (E. Bethge, ed.). New York: Macmillan, 1997.

Boud, D. "The Use of Self-Assessment Schedules in Negotiated Learning." *Studies in Higher Education*, 1992, *17*, 185–200.

Boud, D., Keogh, R., and Walker, D. "Promoting Reflection in Learning: A Model." In D. Boud, R. Keogh, and D. Walker (eds.), *Reflection: Turning Experience into Learning*. East Brunswick, N.J.: Nichols, 1985.

Boud, D., and Walker, D. "Making the Most of Experience." *Studies in Continuing Education*, 1990, *12*, 61–80.

Boud, D., and Walker, D. "Promoting Reflection in Professional Courses: The Challenge of Context." *Studies in Higher Education*, 1998, *23*, 191–206.

Brookfield, S. D. *Developing Critical Thinkers: Challenging Adults to Explore Alternative Ways of Thinking and Acting*. San Francisco: Jossey-Bass, 1987.

Dewey, J. *How We Think: A Restatement of the Relation of Reflective Thinking to the Educative Process*. San Francisco: New Lexington Press, 1933.

Gramsci, A. *Selections from the Prison Notebooks of Antonio Gramsci*. (Q. Hoare and G.-N. Smith, trans.). New York: International Universities Press, 1971.

Mezirow, J., and others. *Fostering Critical Reflection in Adulthood: A Guide to Transformative and Emancipatory Learning*. San Francisco: Jossey-Bass, 1990.

Moon, J. *Reflection in Learning and Professional Development*. London: Kogan Page, 1999a.

Moon, J. *Learning Journals: A Handbook for Academics, Students and Professional Development*. London: Kogan Page, 1999b.

Rainer, T. *The New Diary*. London: Angus and Robertson, 1980.

Schön, D. A. *The Reflective Practitioner: How Professionals Think in Action*. New York: Basic Books, 1983.

Schön, D. A. *Educating the Reflective Practitioner*. San Francisco: Jossey-Bass, 1987.

David Boud is professor of adult education at the University of Technology, Sydney, Australia.

2

Adult educators should consider the benefits of journal writing in terms of their own learning and professional development.

Uses and Benefits of Journal Writing

Roger Hiemstra

Journal writing as an instructional or learning tool in adult education has gained cogency during the past three decades. As early as 1965, psychologist Ira Progoff and his colleagues began seeing the value of personal journals in enhancing growth and learning. Progoff (1975) believed that what he called an "intensive journal process" could "draw each person's life toward wholeness at its own tempo. . . . It systematically evokes and strengthens the inner capacities of persons by working from a non-medical vantage point and proceeding without analytic or diagnostic categories" (p. 9).

Adult educator Malcolm Knowles (1975) introduced readers to notions of personal reflection through activities such as self-assessment and proactive reading of materials. Another useful source is Christensen (1981), who describes how adults can use a diary as a learning tool. Brookfield (1987, 1995) provides various ideas pertaining to critically reflective writing through the use of such tools as autobiography, critical incident citing, and seeing ourselves as others see us.

In spite of more than three decades of use and attempts by a few adult educators to encourage personal reflection in various ways, journaling remains underused as a teaching or learning tool. As a professor, I have found tremendous value in the journaling process for those learners with whom I have interactions. Thus, this chapter reflects not only what others are saying about journal writing but also my own experiences.

Why Use the Journaling Process?

Journaling in its various forms is a means for recording personal thoughts, daily experiences, and evolving insights. The process often evokes conversations with self, another person, or even an imagined other person. When

NEW DIRECTIONS FOR ADULT AND CONTINUING EDUCATION, no. 90, Summer 2001
© John Wiley & Sons, Inc.

we add to this list the advantage available in most journaling formats of being able to review or reread earlier reflections, a progressive clarification of insights is possible.

In the adult education classroom, this learning method becomes a tool to aid learners in terms of personal growth, synthesis, and reflection on new information that they acquire. I urge my learners to use one of the journaling formats as a means for assisting them to obtain the maximum amount of interaction, knowledge, and personal growth from their reading efforts or other learning experiences.

There also is the potential for a journaling technique to promote critical self-reflection where dilemmas, contradictions, and evolving worldviews are questioned or challenged. In the graduate classroom, for example, this may be an especially valued result as teachers attempt to facilitate professional development in their learners. Learning something that is new or different, and then reflecting on what that means for a current or expected professional position, can be an important outcome. Some of my students include portions of a journal or diary in a professional portfolio as a means of demonstrating to current or prospective employers their ability to reflect on issues critically.

I also urge my students to incorporate such self-reflection through a journaling technique into the development of a personal statement of philosophy or a code of personal ethics (Hiemstra, 1999). "This recognition of personal values, beliefs, and the various changes a person undergoes throughout life, if combined with a personal philosophy statement, can result in foundational tools useful as guides or mirrors for subsequent professional action and ethical decision making" (Hiemstra, 1988, p. 178).[1]

Journal Types and Formats

A variety of journaling types and formats have been developed over the years. A literature search produces a plethora of types, descriptions, and examples. Here, I am examining those I have found particularly useful in the graduate classroom. Each has advantages and disadvantages, but all are effective in helping students record information important to their efforts. Most students use journals to move beyond the knowledge and skills available through normal classroom activities. (In Chapter Eight, Jarvis provides other examples of the use of journal writing in higher education.)

Learning Journals. A learning journal typically is a handwritten entry in a notebook or on a pad of paper that records thoughts, reflections, feelings, personal opinions, and even hopes or fears during an educational experience. Students can also use a tape recorder or computer keyboard. The challenge is to find a recording device that feels comfortable and leads to frequent writing. The comments in the learning journal can come from stimulation received while reading course materials or talking with fellow students. They also can be random reflections obtained during a learning experience or just through participation in life. Progoff (1975) suggests having simulated conversations with the inner self or real conversations with others, including obtaining feedback, as a means of furthering ideas received through the process.

Throughout a course, I recommend that students maintain a personal journal, diary, or log to capture in words their growing understanding of the field, a particular subject, and their own professional development. This can include systematic observations of insights, events, and changes in personal perspectives during the course. Journaling, as it is often called, typically is one of the most complex of all forms for recording personal changes and insights. For many students, the process of maintaining a journal helps them to become more organized and focused on the areas they are studying. There is often a bit of personal clarification that takes place as the journaling process helps in the elucidation of opinions, beliefs, and feelings. Progoff (1975) outlines tools or procedures to aid in the writing process, such as personal logs, daily logs, and life history logs.

In my courses, I provide students with a large workbook of supplemental materials. I include a write-up on keeping journals, diaries, reading logs, and theory logs and provide bibliographic references to several supportive sources. I also have on hand a few learning journals and diaries from previous students who have given me permission to share their materials with others needing to look at samples. I also suggest that students search the World Wide Web for samples of journaling forms.

Diaries. A diary is typically a notebook, booklet of blank pages, or any other source for students to record thoughts, reactions to learning experiences, and even innermost fears about a learning activity. Some learners prefer to create electronic or audio diaries. Regardless of the format, entries of daily experiences, insights, and problems often are made. Progoff (1975) writes, "Diary writing usually involves the unstructured, chronological recording of the events of a person's life" as they are perceived. "We have to recognize, however, that the mere fact of continuously writing entries, as is done in the keeping of a diary, is not sufficient in itself to bring about deep changes in a person's life" (p. 87).

Another feature of a diary is being able to look back on specific days or time periods in an attempt to sort out personal feelings. Combining such features with instructor feedback, the development of something like a statement of personal philosophy can begin to take shape. In subsequent writing and reflection, the learner can begin to recognize desired or even unanticipated personal changes as they begin to surface. I recommend that learners read Christensen's (1981) work describing how a personal diary can be used as a supplement to classroom activities.

Dream Book or Log. Many people are interested for personal or psychological reasons in recording and interpreting their dreams. This usually involves keeping a recording device (such as a tablet, notebook, and even tape recorder) on a nightstand to be used for recording the dream experience on wakening before it has faded from conscious memory. Subsequent analysis of those dreams can lead to interpreting how the subconscious might be directing or having some other impact on the conscious. I tell a student who is struggling with some particular concept or subject to consider keeping a dream book or log as a means of obtaining new insights. Bethards (1997) describes how to examine such remembered or recorded symbols from a dream and how to tie them to potentially new understanding or knowledge.

Autobiographies, Life Stories, and Memoirs. Autobiographies, life stories, and memoirs can reveal the heart and soul of human existence. Autobiography focuses on self-assessment, life stories typically assess someone else's life but can be used personally, and memoirs take a more informal approach to telling a life story. All three approaches present an account of someone's life. Something like an autobiography can even be used as a way of understanding or gaining knowledge on a particular topic. For example, a student might arrive at a better understanding of adult development by creating an autobiography that focuses on the various stages of personal development over two or more decades. This typically involves asking students to draw on their own lives and experiences, as well as the lives of others with whom they have associated, and to develop a critical self-reflection on some aspect of their personal development.

In addition to encouraging self-reflection, autobiographies, memoirs, and life stories can promote a sharing of experiences with others by examining similarities and differences between individual life histories. Autobiography thus moves beyond learning as a solitary experience to one based on the potential of synergistic interaction with others.

Spiritual Journals. A spiritual journal usually is somewhat different from a regular journal or diary. It normally involves recording personal reactions to spiritual or religious matters. This particular approach may not match the needs of many adult students, especially if they are taking a course for credit, but occasionally a student with deep religious convictions will find the technique a useful companion to other study activities. Spiritual journals also can be used in retreat settings, where learners use mechanisms to help improve their self-understanding.

Professional Journals. Journals can have a very specific purpose in mind. For example, asking students to keep a professional growth and development journal can be very important, especially as they near the completion of a degree program. Such a journal "may be written solely with the author in mind, or alternatively for a wider professional audience, possibly for colleagues, a tutor, or an assessor in courses in higher education contexts" (O'Hanlon, 1997, p. 168).

I ask my students in their final graduate seminar to keep a professional journal that includes developing a statement of professional commitment (Hiemstra, 1999). The professional journal then becomes part of the learner's professional portfolio, and all these materials are shared with and critiqued by fellow seminar members and me.

Interactive Reading Log. The interactive reading log provides a mechanism for a student to reflect critically on information as it is read. It is essentially a series of reactions or responses to those elements in any material being read that is particularly meaningful or provocative. In essence, learners record aspects of what they are reading in their own voice or words (Perham, 1992). In a graduate course, the items selected for reaction typically include books, instructional media, and professional journal articles.

I recommend to my students that they begin with one or two introductory paragraphs describing the reasons for choosing whatever subject area was covered, include the log of reactions (this could be several pages constituting the bulk of the report), conclude with a two- or three-page retrospective overview of the effort as a whole, and supply a list of references they used. I instruct them to skip some sections in their reading efforts, skim others, read others at a normal rate, or read some passages more carefully and in depth. The spacing and number of reactions depend on the scope and purpose of any reading. It might involve including entire sentences or longer passages that are striking for their clarity, insight, stimulation, and usefulness. It might include items the student regards as ambiguous, exaggerated, poorly reasoned, insufficiently supported, or with which they disagree. They are even encouraged to have simulated conversations with authors as a means of prompting clarification or new insights. The idea is to read and react by letting the experience help in the growth of knowledge and ability to practice critical reflection and as a means of expressing personal thoughts by synthesizing the reading experience.

Theory Log. The assumption serving as a basis for this activity is that each student taking a graduate course will need to learn how to think and reflect critically on corresponding terminology, theory, and knowledge. Brookfield (1995) refers to this activity as reading theory critically. Throughout a learning experience, students who choose to keep a theory log are asked to make notes regarding what they perceive to be theoretical concepts, salient points, truths, bridges to known theory, ideas to be tested, and gaps in the knowledge. They are encouraged to ask epistemological, experiential, communicative, or political questions about what they have read. The ultimate result is a log, statement, outline, or whatever else seems appropriate in expressing their grasp of the theory that will provide a foundation for the course content.

Electronic Journaling. Because of the growing use of computer technology and distance education, many students are choosing to record their insights or reflections in electronic form. In essence, any of the previously described journaling techniques can be carried out fully or partially in an electronic form. One of my students, for example, likes to publish his insights on his Web page for fellow students to read. He subsequently encourages computer-mediated conversations as a way of enhancing his own knowledge and understanding. Some related Web sites can be seen in "Life Journal" (1999) and "My Story" (1998).

Benefits of Journal Writing

There are a number of potential benefits for learners in maintaining some type of journal, diary, or log. For example, most learners show intellectual growth and development, especially as they gain experience with the writing or recording procedures. As a teacher, I have been pleased with how these learning tools can help learners in their personal development and ability to examine new knowledge in critical ways.

Personal Growth and Development. Perhaps most important of all the benefits for the adult learner is the enhancement of personal growth and development. Journaling can help with such learning goals or expected outcomes as integrating life experiences with learning endeavors, allowing for a freedom of expression that may be inhibited in a group setting, stimulating mental development, enhancing breakthroughs in terms of new insights, and even planting seeds of ambition in terms of future study or research. Journal writing is an investment in self through a growing awareness of personal thoughts and feelings.

Intuition and Self-Expression. Another outcome, and one that is not always expected, is an enhanced ability at self-discovery. Learning to trust that inner voice and interpret new thoughts or even dreams can increase self-confidence not only in the classroom but in many other settings. I am immensely satisfied when I see learners tackle new topics because of their growing ability to reflect personally on changes taking place and to integrate such new knowledge into what they already know.

Problem Solving. Using a journaling technique often helps in the solution of problems. Writing down and imagining your way through a problem using personal insights and reflections on life experiences can be rewarding. Often an epiphany emerges that might not have been possible with some other problem-solving technique. I recommend to my students who are engaged in one of the journaling procedures that they allow adequate time in their reflecting processes for new perspectives to emerge.

Stress Reduction and Health Benefits. There is considerable evidence that journaling can improve personal health. Bruce (1998) describes research with subjects who wrote thoughtfully and emotionally about traumatic experiences, and most of them generally experienced improved physical health. Adams (1998) also talks about journaling as therapy for psychological healing and growth. Most adult education students may not need psychotherapy or medical recovery assistance, but some can use whatever helps them to release pent-up emotions, counter anger or frustration, and overcome or reduce the stress so typical in today's busy work world and lifestyle.

Reflection and Critical Thinking. Journaling helps adult learners increase their ability to reflect critically on what they are studying or learning. The resulting outcomes from values clarification, that is, finding meaning in what is being examined, and developing wholeness as a professional through critical judgments enhance not only the professional but also the profession.

Overcoming Writing Blocks

During the journaling process, students typically face an obstacle in not knowing what to do next. In essence, they reach an impasse that can even inhibit their continuing with the writing process. As an instructor, I keep alert for such circumstances through questions I ask in class and in individual advising sessions where I surface potential problems.

Hiemstra and Brier (1994) note that there are various types of blocks: "Some blocks are internal, that is, they reside within the writer. Other blocks are outside the writer and are external in nature" (p. 59). In addition to an obstacle's impact on the journal writing process, it can produce varying degrees of frustration, anxiety, and even enervation.

Although such writing inhibitors can be unsettling, they are part of the process of sorting through new learnings or probing how personal feelings are changing. Progoff (1975) developed a number of techniques to help a person move beyond some blocking issues. Techniques such as imagery work, daily logs, period logs, stepping-stone identification, and even dialogue with fellow learners often help a person to move forward with new insights, reflections, and ideas. Those using an electronic recording mechanism can accomplish the same thing through a chatroom or some form of asynchronous discussion.

Cortright (2000) also describes various approaches to help students move forward with the writing process. These include such techniques as writing quickly, allowing words to fall freely from the subconscious, dating journal entries, using different writing or recording techniques to enhance a feeling of creativity, and setting aside time that is devoted only to the journal or diary writing. In the chapters that follow, the authors provide ideas on how to help learners overcome barriers to learning.

Conclusion

There is considerable evidence of the tremendous benefit possible through a journaling technique. Enhancing the ability of each person to take increasing personal responsibility for personal growth and development is a goal that has tremendous potential by encouraging a "proactive approach to the learning process" (Brockett and Hiemstra, 1991, p. 27).

Note

1. Several journaling techniques, types, and formats have been tailored to fit my particular instructional philosophy and approach, so you may need to make appropriate adjustments if you decide to use them in your own classroom (Hiemstra and Sisco, 1990). For additional material related to many of the techniques, see Hiemstra (2000).

References

Adams, K. *The Way of the Journal: A Journey Therapy Workbook for Healing.* (2nd ed.) Towson, Md.: Sidran Press, 1998.

Bethards, B. *The Dream Book: Symbols for Self-Understanding.* (Rev. ed.) Boston: Element Books, 1997.

Brockett, R. G., and Hiemstra, R. *Self-Direction in Adult Learning: Perspectives on Theory, Research, and Practice.* New York: Routledge, 1991.

Brookfield, S. D. *Developing Critical Thinkers: Challenging Adults to Explore Alternative Ways of Thinking and Acting.* San Francisco: Jossey-Bass, 1987.

Brookfield, S. D. *Becoming a Critically Reflective Teacher.* San Francisco: Jossey-Bass, 1995.

Bruce, R. "Strange But True: Improve Your Health Through Journaling." [www.shpm.com/articles/health/journal.html]. May 1998.

Christensen, R. S. "Dear Diary—A Learning Tool for Adults." *Lifelong Learning: The Adult Years,* 1981, 5, 4–5, 23.

Cortright, S. M. "Journaling: A Tool for the Spirit." [housewifemagazine.com/scape/Journaling.html]. Mar. 2000.

Hiemstra, R. "Translating Personal Values and Philosophy into Practical Action." In R. G. Brockett (ed.), *Ethical Issues in Adult Education.* New York: Teachers College Press, 1988.

Hiemstra, R. "Ethics and the Adult Educator." [home.twcny.rr.com/hiemstra/ethics.html]. Jan. 1999.

Hiemstra, R. "Techniques, Tools, and Resources for the Self-Directed Learner." [home.twcny.rr.com/hiemstra/sdltools.html]. Mar. 2000.

Hiemstra, R., and Brier, E. *Professional Writing: Processes, Strategies, and Tips for Publishing in Educational Journals.* Malabar, Fla.: Krieger, 1994.

Hiemstra, R., and Sisco, B. *Individualizing Instruction: Making Learning Personal, Empowering, and Successful.* San Francisco: Jossey-Bass, 1990.

Knowles, M. S. *Self-Directed Learning.* New York: Association Press, 1975.

"Life Journal." [www.lifejournal.com/adams.html]. 1999.

"My Story: The Complete Autobiography Writer System." [www.mystorywriter.com/home.htm]. 1998.

O'Hanlon, C. "The Professional Journal, Genres and Personal Development in Higher Education." In S. Hollingsworth (ed.), *International Action Research: A Casebook for Educational Reform.* Bristol, Pa.: Falmer Press, 1997.

Perham, A. J. "Collaborative Journals." Paper presented at the National Council of Teachers of English Conference, 1992. (ED 355 555)

Progoff, I. *At a Journal Workshop.* New York: Dialogue House Library, 1975.

Roger Hiemstra is professor of adult education, Elmira College, Elmira, New York.

3

This chapter uses cases to explore ethical questions in journal writing and provides principles for using it in educational settings.

Ethical Concerns Relating to Journal Writing

Leona M. English

Much of the concern of adult educators about ethics has centered on whether there should be a code of ethics. This focus of attention has veered the discussion away from the essential topic of ethical concerns and has concentrated deliberations on the professionalization of the field of adult education. The consequence has been the neglect of vital concerns and a divide between those who argue for a code or ethics (Connelly and Light, 1991; McDonald and Wood, 1993; Robertson, 1996) and those who argue against one (Cunningham, 1992; Sisco, 1988). I believe that the central question is not whether we have a code but, rather, how can we become thoughtful, critically reflective adult educators who raise ethical questions regarding decision making relating to practice. No code can make us more ethical or reflective; a code can only provide sanctions for violators. Arguably, a case can be made that sufficient sanctions exist in the field without these being codified. In this chapter, I leave aside the structural issues relating to codes and move to the heart of the matter: asking questions that move us closer to our basic human orientation toward the good. In other words, "in order to make minimal sense of our lives, in order to have an identity, we need an orientation to the good" (Taylor, 1989, p. 47). As I see it, ethical questions move adult educators closer to this good.

Adult Educators and Ethics

One could argue that more and more attention is being devoted to ethical issues in adult education. Brookfield (1998), who has been writing about moral learning, points out that "adult educators like to think of themselves

NEW DIRECTIONS FOR ADULT AND CONTINUING EDUCATION, no. 90, Summer 2001
© John Wiley & Sons, Inc.

as moral beings" (p. 283). This concern with contributing to the common good and living morally has been important for adult educators for a long time, though interest seems to have ebbed and waned. During the early years of the field of adult education, ethical concerns for the common good impelled pioneers like Lindeman (1961), Coady (1939), Horton (Horton, Peters, Gaventa, and Bell, 1990), and Corbett (1957), who heralded these concerns. Lindeman, for instance, urged adult educators to be active in social change. He argued that "adult education will become an agency of progress if its short-time goal of self-improvement can be made compatible with a long-time, experimental but resolute policy of changing the social order" (p. 105).

Unfortunately, the field more recently has moved in the direction of professionalization and humanism. The concern for the common good has not claimed center stage, as early adult educators had hoped it would. A discussion of ethical issues today can help to rekindle some of the early ideas and reframe our conversation so that it is more focused on the common good. An encouraging piece of research is that of Daloz, Keen, Keen, and Parks (1996), who studied how adults deal daily with questions of the common good. From their interviews with one hundred American adults, whose lives demonstrate commitment to the betterment of their community (the common good), they found out how the interviewers made ethical choices and what factors influenced their choices. These adults were not heroes in the ordinary sense of the word, but each one demonstrated the ability to make wise choices and orient their lives toward the improvement of others. In many ways, this chapter is a response to this call for developing an ethics of adult education that focuses attention on and is oriented to the other (see also Jarvis, 1997).

Merriam and Caffarella (1998) have drawn attention to a variety of ethical frameworks in adult education, especially the ethic of care. Gilligan (1982), too, has highlighted this ethic in her work on moral reasoning. The ethic of care stresses relationship and interdependence as the basis for ethical decision making. A caring relationship, influenced by elements of an ethics of justice or critique, often becomes the criterion by which decisions are made. Those who value or are influenced by an ethic of care may be more likely to choose journal writing as a vehicle to enhance and support their learning. An ethic of care will also influence how educators assess journals and how they view the importance of a personal dimension in journal entries. An ethic of care will influence the quality of the relationship between the educator and the learner, that is, the one who writes the journal, and it will also help to shape the lens by which the educator views themes of ultimate concern to all learners.

Ethical issues and concerns must be part of any discussion and practice of adult education. Ethics challenges reflective practitioners in the field of adult education to think about, and consider seriously, the issues that arise in the facilitation of any experiential learning methods like journal writing. Although the word *ethics* is often used in relation to problems that need to be solved, the sense in which I use it in this chapter is not problem based. From my perspective, all of life raises ethical questions, running the broad gamut of how we treat learners and ourselves to how we decide to eliminate trash from our computer's bin.

Generalized Concerns About Journal Writing

Despite the complexity of ethical behavior, educators believe that ethics can be taught. The evidence for this fact is that ethics courses are offered routinely in professional programs such as business, medicine, education, and nursing and in subject areas such as anthropology and sociology. The underlying assumption is that those who take part in these courses will continue to raise ethical problems and issues relating to their profession and will engage in dialogue about these with their coworkers.

One good example of an ethical issue is the use of experiential learning strategies such as journal writing. Educators in a variety of settings are concerned about its use. For example, sociologists, who are increasingly using experiential learning methods (Grauerholz and Copenhaver, 1994), raise questions about the intersection of the personal and the professional in a learning environment. English and Lander (2000) have discussed how journals can be used advantageously in distance education and caution about its use. Similarly, McKee (1999), an anthropologist, has discussed the use of journal writing in anthropology courses delivered at a distance and shared issues relating to its use. Adult educators with concerns about journal writing continuously engage in dialogue about these issues (see Kerka, 1996).

Ethical Issues Relating to Journal Writing

There are many issues relating to the use of journal writing, not the least of which is how to balance the integration of the personal and professional. Another issue is the assessment of journal writing.

The Personal and the Professional. Elbow and Clarke (1987) note that the fear of who will read the journal is often a problem for those who engage in journal writing. They argue that whether someone reads the journal or not, the question of audience is hard to ignore. In their opinion, it is easier to engage in journal writing if the writers ignore the audience or "readers who will judge their writing" (p. 23). This issue of audience speaks to the intersection of the personal and the professional and raises ethical questions about this intersection. The dilemma this issue poses is whether the practice of crossing boundaries between the intersections has integrity. Many would respond that the personal and the professional cannot be separated because they are at the heart of the adult education and meaning-making interstices. Many believe that if the two are separated, the possibility for holistic education will be ignored. In fact, the postmodern thrust in adult education acknowledges and welcomes such tensions and boundary crossings. Postmodernism accepts and respects disjunctures such as the intersection of the personal and the professional. (Fenwick discusses similar issues of readership and response in Chapter Four.)

The intrusion on the lifeworld of adults raises an intriguing question for adult educators who decide to use journal writing with their students. In this regard, Boud and Walker (1998) allege that there can be inappropriate levels of self-disclosure in journal writing, as in any other type of reflective exercise. They claim that the shift to reflective practice, especially by those influenced by the bandwagon effect, has led to an uncritical acceptance and promotion of reflective exercises in learning. Sometimes these reflective activities are reduced to a recipe-like prescription. Boud and Walker caution adult educators to avoid demanding that learners reflect on critical incidents in their lives or ask learners for too much disclosure, especially when there are inadequate support services to counsel learners in crisis.

Boud and Walker (1998) believe that adult educators who promote reflectivity need to analyze the culture in which they teach carefully and critically before they introduce reflective exercises. A competency-based learning environment, for instance, may not provide an optimal environment for reflective activities, nor would an institution that has a poor track record with regard to human rights be a useful one in which to pursue rights of gender and sexual orientation. They suggest that consideration of the culture of the organization will be a good indicator of the level of possibilities for reflection. They stress the importance of knowing the discipline's boundaries, the context, and the possibilities for reflection.

Ultimately, educators must ask themselves how much they agree with Henry David Thoreau's statement that journals are "of myself, for myself." Their answer will help them to decide how to go about balancing a need for privacy with the practice of reflection in their educational setting. The issue of audience with respect to journal writing is perhaps the most serious ethical question confronting adult education today.

The Ethics of Assessment. In many adult education settings such as in higher education and literacy instruction, the instructor reads and assesses learners' journals. This reality presents major ethical issues that are well worth considering. The fact that an instructor will read the journal may inhibit some learners from writing what is on their minds or from engaging in meaningful writing, reflecting, and learning. Consequently, the depth of the learning that is possible is often impeded.

Boud and Walker (1998) pose a key question: Are journals to be judged by criteria for reflective writing or by some other standard? This query demands that as a first step, adult educators must decide how journal entries will be assessed. One way of assessing journals is to use Hatton and Smith's (1995) framework. They distinguish several levels of reflective writing. The first level, descriptive, is not reflective; rather, it is a mere listing of events that occurred and without any explanation. The second level, descriptive reflection, describes the events that took place, provides some explanation, and considers alternative courses of action. The third level of reflection, dialogic reflection, includes stepping back from an event in order to think about various alternatives, possibilities, and courses of action. This level also includes analysis of events. The last level requires critical reflection, that is, an awareness that events are influenced by multiple historical events and are situated in a social-political context. This last level requires an ability to do structural assessment.

From the outset, the adult educator needs to be clear about journal entries—in other words, what is required and what is acceptable. Providing guidelines for the learner about what is expected, the depth of writing and the intent of the writing, is very important in establishing an ethical basis for teaching and learning. Guidelines also make clear the amount of personal integration that is required. However, not all adult educators agree that journal writing can be assessed. Brookfield (1995), for instance, says that the material presented in a journal entry is, and should be, nonassessable. Whether the adult educator agrees with this view is an important decision to make before negotiating a journal writing assignment as part of any course requirements.

Ethical Problems in Practice

When an adult educator decides to use journals, many ethical issues arise. To illustrate the difficulty of using journal writing as part of a course or program, I provide several examples here. Each example presents ethical issues, and, flowing from these, some questions to ponder. The reader is invited to add other questions.

- Case 1. A nursing instructor asks her students in the last year of their bachelor of nursing program to begin keeping a journal. One of them uses her journal as a vehicle to report that another student has been cheating on examinations. This information poses several questions: Are the journals private and personal? Is it ethical to use information taken from a private journal? Because the student had used the journal for a purpose that was unintended—in this case, to report on the conduct of another student—does the instructor have the right or the obligation to do anything about the student who was accused of cheating? What other issues does this situation raise?
- Case 2. In a manufacturing company, a workplace instructor has been offering a literacy class to employees who have low levels of literacy. This company is attempting to unionize, and management has asked the administrator of the workplace education division to find out the names of those who have been organizing the union. The administrator decides to snoop in the instructor's office, where he discovers some student journals. He reads the journals to find out if some of the employees taking

part in the literacy class have been part of the organizing effort. In this case, how do the issues of power and the violation of personal rights become reconciled? What other issues does this case raise?

- Case 3. A university professor who teaches in a distance-education program writes responses week after week in a student's journal. She is troubled by the fact that the student is isolated from the university and is limited to her comments. The voice, opinions, and points of view of the whole class or the larger intellectual community are not accessible to this student (see McKee, 1999). The professor questions whether journal writing is a legitimate academic experience, especially in a distance-education program. Should the student be given feedback by other people or have the opportunity to interact with other learners? The isolation and the narrowness of the student's education greatly concerns her. She asks herself, "Is this an ethical issue?" If so, what should she do? What do others do, who feel the same way?

- Case 4. A social work student in a continuing-education program writes confidential comments in her learning journal about family child abuse cases that she is involved in at her workplace. Although she has disguised the case somewhat, it is difficult to establish complete anonymity. When the instructor responds to a pile of journals, some pages from this student's work accidentally become mixed with those of another student. Consequently, only half of the student's assignment is returned. She becomes alarmed because the confidential information has disappeared. Unfortunately, the instructor's best efforts to retrieve the lost pages have not been successful. What happens when the confidential information in one journal, in this case, a child abuse situation, ends up in another student's hands? How can confidentiality be ensured?

The four cases are all different, but each one points out the difficulty of establishing guidelines for the use of journals in adult education. They also highlight the fact that the intersection of professional and personal information is not easy and at times makes the situation difficult to negotiate. They highlight as well the intricacies of the adult education task of responding to and assessing journal entries.

Principles to Govern the Use of Journal Writing

The following guidelines, based on Brockett's (1990) discussion of ethical principles, can help adult educators who use journal writing in their practice.

- *Respect.* The educator needs to ask first and foremost, How can I implement journal writing in such a way that I respect the students with whom I work? This principle puts the learner's best interests first and makes confidentiality and boundary setting essential characteristics of a journal writing exercise. This principle ensures that there are no major obstacles to a student's privacy.

- *Justice.* This principle ensures that there is equity in service to learners. One way that this principle is put in practice is to ensure that journals submitted for assessment are responded to in a reasonable time. This principle ensures that adult educators who use journal writing in their courses focus on journals as learning tools, not as vehicles for therapy. The purpose of the journal based on this principle is to assist in learning knowledge, skills, and attitudes.
- *Beneficence* (promoting good). This principle means that the learners' opportunities for positive outcomes are maximized. A good way to operationalize this principle when the journal writing is assigned is for the educator to ask, Are harmful outcomes minimized and positive outcomes maximized? Do I guard the journal entries and make sure these are not shared with others? Do I treat journal entries with the utmost respect? Am I using journals as a way to increase the potential for learning?
- *Self-awareness.* This principle, perhaps the most challenging, is one of mutuality. It requests educators, provided they are willing and ready, to do what they have asked their students to do. Are they willing to engage in a process of reflection on their own adult education practice? If they are, adult educators must keep a journal and share their experiences of the process (not necessarily the content) of the journal writing if they are to model reflective practice for their learners. It is important to the integrity of the process if educators do what they expect of the student.
- *Caring.* This principle requires educators to think seriously about whether they really care about the students with whom they work. Caring will be evident in a clear demarcation of roles and expectations. This happens when adult educators inform students from the outset about the purpose of journal writing, provide guidelines for the task, and explain how the journals will be evaluated. The assessment process should be clearly defined, especially in terms of what the teacher will or will not read.

The ultimate ethical question is whether we are committed to our own ethical practice and to evaluating our own learning and living out of the questions that arise out of our practice. Noddings's (1992) ethic of care applies here. As she points out, one of the main ways that we can bring ethical concerns to our teaching is by working on our own practice through journal writing and the practice of critical reflection. To be effective educators, we need to be reflective practitioners ourselves. This requirement poses a tantalizing question: Am I also engaged in my own reflective practice, or is this what I require my students to do?

Conclusion

As the poet Rilke (1984) suggests, we need not search vainly for answers, but rather try to "love the questions themselves" (p. 34). This chapter is a good example; it has raised more questions than it has provided easy answers. It is a fact of life that ethical questions cannot escape us as thinking human beings. In other words, the study of ethical concerns depends on our willingness to engage in the lifelong work of constructing meaning from our experiences, work, and relationships, either in our worklife or our home life. From this perspective, ethics is viewed as the lifelong quest to know more deeply and intimately what is good, right, and valuable. Ethics challenges our thinking, feeling, and willing capacities and challenges us to become more critical, more wondering, and more questioning.

Ethical questions cannot be trivialized. They are important issues for adult educators, and they arise every time we discuss an issue, put something into practice, engage in dialogue with colleagues, and interact with learners. The use of journal writing raises a great number of questions, mainly because it involves personal issues. However, there are many areas of ethics not covered in this chapter, including the notions of gender, environment, and equity. Adult educators need to challenge themselves by asking questions about their practice, deeply considering the implications of their actions, and putting the learners' needs at the center of their decision making.

References

Boud, D., and Walker, D. "Promoting Reflection in Professional Courses: The Challenge of Context." *Studies in Higher Education,* 1998, 23, 191–206.

Brockett, R. G. "Adult Education: Are We Doing It Ethically?" *Mountain Plains Adult Education Association Journal of Adult Education,* 1990, 19, 5–12.

Brookfield, S. *Becoming a Critically Reflective Teacher.* San Francisco: Jossey-Bass, 1995.

Brookfield, S. "Understanding and Facilitating Moral Learning in Adults." *Journal of Moral Education,* 1998, 27, 283–300.

Coady, M. *Masters of Their Own Destiny.* New York: HarperCollins, 1939.

Connelly, R. J., and Light, K. M. "An Interdisciplinary Code of Ethics for Adult Education." *Adult Education Quarterly,* 1991, 41, 233–240.

Corbett, E. A. *We Have with Us Tonight.* Toronto: Ryerson Press, 1957.

Cunningham, P. M. "Adult Education Does Not Need a Code of Ethics." In M. W. Galbraith and B. R. Sisco (eds.), *Confronting Controversies in Challenging Times: A Call for Action.* New Directions for Adult and Continuing Education, no. 54. San Francisco: Jossey-Bass, 1992.

Daloz, L.A.P., Keen, C. H., Keen, J. P., and Parks, S. D. *Common Fire: Leading Lives of Commitment in a Complex World.* Boston: Beacon Press, 1996.

Elbow, P., and Clark, J. "Desert Island Discourse: The Benefits of Ignoring Audience." In T. Fulwiler (ed.), *The Journal Book.* Portsmouth, N.H.: Boynton/Cook, 1987.

English, L. M., and Lander, D. "Increasing Reflection and Dialogue in Distance Learning." *Journal for the Art of Teaching,* 2000, 7, 85–95.

Gilligan, C. *In a Different Voice: Psychological Theory and Women's Development.* Cambridge, Mass.: Harvard University Press, 1982.

Grauerholz, E., and Copenhaver, S. "When the Personal Becomes Problematic: The Ethics of Using Experiential Teaching Methods." *Teaching Sociology,* 1994, 22, 319–327.

Hatton, N., and Smith, D. "Reflection in Teacher Education: Towards Definition and Implementation." *Teaching and Teacher Education,* 1995, 11, 33–49.

Horton, M., Peters, J. M., Gaventa, J., and Bell, B. *We Make the Road by Walking: Conversations on Education and Social Change.* Philadelphia: Temple University Press, 1990.

Jarvis, P. *Ethics and Education for Adults in a Late Modern Society*. London: National Institute for Adult Continuing Education, 1997.

Kerka, S. *Journal Writing and Adult Learning*. Columbus, Ohio: Clearinghouse on Adult, Career, and Vocational Education, 1996. (ED 399 413)

Lindeman, E. C. *The Meaning of Adult Education*. New York: Continuum, 1961. (Originally published 1926.)

McDonald, K. S., and Wood, G. S. "Surveying Adult Education Practitioners About Ethical Issues." *Adult Education Quarterly*, 1993, *43*, 243–257.

McKee, N. "The Great Conversation at a Distance: Using Journals in an Anthropology Telecourse." *American Journal of Distance Education*, 1999, *13*, 62–72.

Merriam, S., and Caffarella, R. *Learning in Adulthood: A Comprehensive Guide*. (2nd ed.) San Francisco: Jossey-Bass, 1998.

Noddings, N. *The Challenge to Care in Schools: An Alternative Approach to Education*. New York: Teachers College Press, 1992.

Rilke, M. R. "Letter 4." In *Letters to a Young Poet*. (S. Mitchell, trans.). New York: Random House, 1984.

Robertson, D. L. "Facilitating Transformative Learning: Attending to the Dynamics of the Educational Helping Relationship." *Adult Education Quarterly*, 1996, *47*, 41–53.

Sisco, B. R. "Dilemmas in Continuing Education Administration." In R. Brockett (ed.), *Ethical Issues in Adult Education*. New York: Teachers College Press, 1988.

Taylor, C. *Sources of the Self: The Making of the Modern Identity*. Cambridge, Mass.: Harvard University Press, 1989.

Leona M. English is associate professor of adult education at Saint Francis Xavier University, Antigonish, Nova Scotia.

4

Responders to journals can exert a powerful influence on the writer's experience and learning process. Response can balance caring, intuitive listening with rigorous inquiry in a meaningful dialogue.

Responding to Journals in a Learning Process

Tara J. Fenwick

"If I have to do one more journal I'm going to throw up." A graduate student of mine in a burst of frustration claimed she was required to keep three journals simultaneously in different classes. Her comment prompted me to pause and rethink, with considerable humility, the whole point of assigning and responding to learners' journal writings.

Journal writing is a convention in adult education, and it has been a staple of my own teaching and research practice for twenty years. I have been a lifelong journal writer myself and early in my career supposed that everyone else would discover the liberating imaginative landscapes, the head-cleaning emotional releases, and the sometimes intoxicating glimpses of clarity that await the intrepid journal writer. But after some disillusionment and considerable adjustment in my views on journal writing, I gradually evolved a variety of methods for using journal writing with adult learners. I found ways to introduce journals gently to newcomers, coaxing the hesitant and encouraging and sustaining initial efforts. I recognized that new journal writers want to sense a genuine listener at the other end of their writing. I discovered that journal writers sometimes land in frustrating craters of "stuckness." In response, I tried offering questions or anecdotes from my own experience to help learners get unstuck or at least feel reassured that others too hit these swampy bogs from time to time. I tried to find ways to respond frequently and parsimoniously to learners' journal writing without losing whole weekends buried in stacks of intimate scribblings. But I also found that writers sometimes just need to be left alone, neither wanting nor benefiting from some responder's intrusion.

NEW DIRECTIONS FOR ADULT AND CONTINUING EDUCATION, no. 90, Summer 2001
© John Wiley & Sons, Inc.

Learners signaled key areas of discomfort, challenging me to develop new ways of responding as a helpful audience. Some learners sought more outside direction, and I tried to give them permission to be more self-directed. Others got bogged down in what I thought to be excessively personal and subjective venting or a sort of superficial rambling, which they admitted left them feeling aimless and dissatisfied with their journal writing. I tried different ways to guide writers around obstacles they perceived, sometimes suggesting topics or creating journal writing starters (questions or controversial issues inviting positions) and sometimes confronting, probing, and prompting, or just affirming. My continuing personal struggle with respect to journal writing balances on a tightrope of author(ity) over what to write and how to write it, balancing my direction with a learner's freedom.

Beyond all else, I learned how careful responders must be in phrasing tonal responses to learners' journal writing. A brief remark meant as light irony can be taken seriously and cause hurt. An honest question from a stance of, "I'm interested in this too," can be interpreted as pointing out the writer's lack of development. Once I wrote "Bingo!" beside a writer's perceptive conclusion, and she thought I was making fun of her. I think I have since learned how to respond caringly with fewer words. Writers can easily get overwhelmed by responses. Some students told me that the most valuable responses were the places where I simply noted an idea as being truly thought provoking for me as the reader, an approach I borrowed from Peter Elbow (1981).

I also discovered, embarrassingly late in my teaching career, the value of sharing journal writing, using it as a springboard in small-group discussions and having learners read and respond to each other's journal writing. One year I overcame my worry about ruining students' idiosyncratic experimentation with form by presenting journal writing models when I introduced the journal writing assignment. I extracted samples of past students' journal writing to share with whole classes. I was surprised at the veritable flood of relief and new understandings ("Oh, *now* I get the hang of this!"), and the subsequent fluency and letting go from some writers who had previously seemed stubbornly taciturn. Journal samples, I discovered, almost always prompted lively discussions about the issue addressed in the sample or the thinking process that the journal writer used. A journal writer's views in a sample about course content and issues seemed to speak directly to other students more powerfully—certainly in language, stance, and context perhaps closer to their own—than course readings. Seemingly, learners do not perceive the same closed authority of text in each others' journal writing that they sometimes attribute to articles and books comprising the course reading list. They often respond to another's journal opinion by respecting, building on, probing, and questioning to inquire and then to challenge. Another big step I took was offering, very hesitantly, my own rough writing in all its rawness and exploratory naivete. I was learning how to listen to the bluntly honest responses that learners offered me through discussion and more journal writing responses.

Following is a compendium of understandings and suggestions gleaned from my own practice about responding humanly and effectively to a learner's journal writing. I offer them humbly but with full enthusiasm. I believe in the power of the journal writing process for learning and change and the value of a responder in that process.

The Nature of the Responsive Relationship

Although journal writing is a private activity, often conducted without any prompting by those particularly drawn to reflective writing, I believe a responder can assist in three ways. First, responders can affirm and thus motivate the journal writing activity. Many adults report that although they valued regular journal writing in a course as a useful learning discipline and fully intended to continue with it, they found it difficult to stay motivated with no incentive such as a responder. Second, responders can assist journal writers to see in the writing what they have missed or overlooked. The journal writer's private world can spiral inside itself without breaking through accustomed patterns of thinking, and journal writers may be unable to clarify insights emerging in their writing. Effective responses can shine new light or simply startle journal writers into enough distance to discern their reflections. Third, good responders enter conversation with the journal writer by probing, extending, and connecting. Berthoff (1987) talks about feedback and "feedforward" in journal writing. Responders enhance the discursive, heuristic power of language itself because their presence can inspire journal writers to express and clarify their ideas for an audience. What for some journal writers is uncomfortable solitude can become a meaningful exchange of ideas. A responder contributes to the dialogue by helping to make thought explicit, develop problem solving, create connections, extend ideas, and discover and validate the self. The important difference between responding to journal writing and exchanging letters is that the journal writer remains in the foreground. The responder is not an equal partner in the conversation, but rather focuses on the writer's process and purposes instead of his or her own interests.

Modes of Response

For journal writing developed in an educational context, there are at least three possible responders: a learner's peers, a supervisor or facilitator of learning, and the learner himself or herself. These possibilities offer advantages and disadvantages, are suitable in particular contexts, and may be combined in a journal writing experience.

Peer as Responder. Journal swapping with a peer or colleague may be appropriate in a mentoring, coaching, or consulting relationships; a work or family relationship; or an educational program. Writers may opt to share the whole journal or selected parts. Peer responders initially may be uncomfortable, not knowing where to start in reading another's personal free-style writing. They may be reluctant or unable to offer challenging questions, probes, extensions, or personal response, yet they often learn much from each other's reflections and perspectives about issues they both encounter.

Instructor as Responder. Instructors, facilitators, and sometimes work supervisors usually respond to journal writing in a process of formative assessment. The danger is offering judgmental comment rather than personal or probing response: the former can shut down free exploratory writing, while the latter celebrates and encourages this kind of writing. Although responders may have insights and perspectives that can assist the writer, they also may have difficulty building the necessary trust in the responsive relationship. The responder's task is to accept and appreciate the writing, affirm the writer and the process, and share in turn. Some responders reciprocate the journal writer's stories by including personal thoughts in their responses. Others keep journals themselves and regularly share relevant sections with learners. This helps create some reciprocity, with the added benefits of modeling the importance of journal writing, demonstrating ways of journaling, and alerting the responder to the difficulties and serendipities of the journal writing process.

A responsive relationship builds over time. As the journal writer develops trust in the responder's appreciation and care for the writing, and grows accustomed to the responder's voice in dialogue, a dialogue gradually develops. The privilege of being invited to read and respond to someone else's journal carries important responsibility. The responder must respect the writing and endeavor to understand, engage, and finally express helpful response in ways that are honest and minimally invasive. Good responders maintain the confidentiality of the writing and appreciate the sometimes chaotic and raw nature of the writing in the first draft. This is why some journal exchange is recommended over one-way modes of response: two journal writers sharing writing with one other develop an implicit sense of mutual vulnerability and care.

Self as Responder. Journal writers might need encouragement to become their own respondents. Some writers reread and comment on their own past writing as a matter of course. Others do not think to do so without prompting. Responders can help writers find a focus for rereading and analyzing their own exploratory writing or appreciate their past voice from the perspective of the present. Berthoff (1999) calls for more attention to close reading and authors' interpretation of their own interpretations to avoid misreading and oversimplified interpretation. Some specific suggestions follow for encouraging journal writers to respond to their own writing. In some contexts, especially when journal writers document intensely private experiences, it may be inappropriate for there to be any responder other than the writer.

Roles of Response

Within the three modes of response—peer, facilitator or supervisor, or self—are different possible roles through which to listen and respond to a journal writer's exploratory writing:

- *As a comforter.* The responder affirms and bolsters the writer's strengths and interests, counters self put-downs, and sometimes offers insight about larger structural issues contributing to a problem the journal writer assumes to be self-contained.
- *As a mirror.* The responder reflects the writer's own themes, recurring images and questions, and gems of thought that appear throughout the journal. Sometimes simply selecting and noting these with a brief comment is sufficient to be helpful.
- *As a provoker.* The responder offers challenges and critical questions, perhaps drawing attention to faulty logic or gaps in thinking, pointing out contradictions in different parts of the writing, or commenting on assumptions contained in the writer's metaphors. This role must be played gently and carefully, and usually only with the writer's permission. Critical commentary without mutual trust can block further writing.
- *As a learning director.* The responder notes conclusions or potential lessons from experience that are emerging in the writing, perhaps suggesting application or implications for further learning. Or the responder may draw attention to the change over the course of the journal itself, perhaps offering language to assist the writer to see the learning process unfolding.
- *As a friend-in-dialogue.* The responder simply extends conversational response, commenting on parts the responder can relate to or agrees with and why, parts that are puzzling, personal stories in kind the responder is stimulated to share by the journal, and even advice.
- *As an evaluator.* The responses offer constructive assistance to help sharpen the writer's thinking, writing, or learning as recorded in the journal, according to specific criteria that have been made clear at the beginning of the process.
- *As a biographer.* The responder creates or shows the story of a life that has emerged in the journal and points out the ways in which the story has been specifically constructed according to a frame of values and assumptions. In other words, the responder opens the door for "re-storying" of the narrative.

Choices among these roles depend on the journal's purpose, the journal writer's intentions and needs, and the responder's relationship with the journal writer. In all cases, responders should approach their task delicately, as invited guests in another's world, appreciating the gift of another's personal writing, and desiring to give in return.

Issues of Confession and Power in Journal Response

Whatever the approach, the reaction of any responder to a private piece of exploratory writing is intrusive. A power relationship is created, potentially subverting a learner's interests to the will of a judging other. The very submission of a learning journal for response forces an individual to reflect in particular ways and times that are convenient to the responder. And in personal writing, as Foucault (1980) points out, the individual is rendered visible and thus subjected to the surveillance and regulation of an evaluator. Usher and Edwards (1995) extend this argument to criticize journal writing as a "confessional" educational practice because it requires humans to turn on themselves as objects, constructing and confessing a self that conforms to culturally approved personal issues and categories of identity. These critiques are useful in understanding the oppressive potential of response when it seeks to normalize, confine, or disempower writers rather than develop relationships of respect. (Chapter Three, on ethical concerns, raised some of these issues.)

The Responder's Balancing Act

The responder also must balance direction and freedom in assisting the writer. If the responder offers too many comments or suggestions, writers may become overwhelmed, losing their own voices or the opportunity to work through a thinking dilemma themselves. If the responder offers too little, writers seeking guidance may be frustrated. Newman (1991) compares the responder's balancing act to flying a kite. There is some preparation and effort at the beginning to get the kite aloft; then the responder must let go. The connection remains through one thin string of response, except when the kite is in trouble and needs rescuing. Otherwise, the kite follows gusts of wind that it meets on its own, far away from the gaze of the responder.

Sometimes journal writing contains revelations that are highly intimate, personal, and entirely unrelated to the journal's purpose. Such entries may be a desperate cry for help, an appeal to be understood as a human being, an attempt to form an alliance, a way to vent negative feelings, or perhaps a desire to shock. Ignoring certain entries seems to be a cold betrayal of trust, but responding directly may open a therapeutic relationship that is entirely inappropriate given the responder's level of experience and may ultimately disempower the writer. Effective response demands intuition, attention to context and purpose, understanding of the journal writer's needs and the responder's role, a commitment to caring, and a balance between boundaries and openness to exploration. Response is rarely clear-cut.

Suggestions for Responders

There are many ways to respond to another's journal writing in respectful dialogue. One way is to craft responses that enhance the journal's purpose and the writer's experience developing the journal. Suggestions for descriptive personal response follow. If journal writing is to be submitted in its entirety to another reader, whether a peer or facilitator, writers must be made aware of this fact before they begin writing. For situations where journal writing is required, as part of a course, then submitted for assessment as well as response, suggestions for grading are provided here. The issue of disclosure to a facilitator needs to be managed sensitively. Where journal writing is a confessional record that tracks a period of personal growth, it is probably inappropriate for a responder even to read the learner's writing. It is certainly unfair to place a grade on such personal writing. In these cases, partial assessment or self-assessment may be approaches to consider.

Descriptive Personal Response. Descriptive response should be given whenever a learner's journal writing is submitted to a reader. A learner has extended the trust of sharing personal writing with another human being. Only an insensitive or rushed responder would respond simply with a numeric grade. With learners who are using journal writing for the first time, responses should be given early in the process to help guide and focus their writing.

In determining what comments are most helpful, think of responding personally, honestly, openly, and humanly. What you say and how far you nudge writers depends on meeting them where they are and sensing where they want to move. Listen carefully to the writer's questions and the currents that may be flowing beneath the words. Above all, be present and honor the writer. Responders sometimes offer tidbits of their own experience to help a learner feel more comfortable with personal writing. Sometimes they write questions in the margins or point out a focus to help the writer develop a particular line of thinking. Some write comments of encouragement or show the learner which parts of the journal writing strike the responder as insightful or powerful. Some write nothing in the journal pages and instead write a personal letter to the learner at the end of the journal writing. Here are some further specific suggestions for responding to learner journal writing (Kirby and Liner, 1988, pp. 68–70):

"Be an *active* reader."
"Encourage the student to share excerpts from the journal writing with classmates."
"Suggest future topics. Notice profitable digressions."
"Ask for permission to publish good stuff to share with other students."
"Write an extended response, a short poem, or ask questions.
"Avoid empty comments like 'interesting,' 'nice,' or 'good idea.'"
"Be honest with students."
"Look for something good."
"Avoid sarcasm." Even offhand humorous comments in writing can be hurtful.
"Take a break." Respond to just a few journals at a time.

Responding to Evaluate. Journal writing can be read and responded to without being given a grade. In graded courses, some responders grant automatic credit to learners who complete a journal writing requirement, say 10 to 20 percent of a course grade. Alternatively, responders may evaluate journal writing holistically, skim-reading the whole thing or parts marked for reading by the learner, and rate the overall journal writing on a three- or five-point scale according to specific criteria. These criteria must spring from the journal writing's purpose, must be provided to the writers, and must be clarified throughout the writing period. Exhibit 4.1 is an example of a five-point scale that might be adapted to generate a holistic grade on journal writing. Responders should ask writers to submit personally chosen samples rather than whole journals only.

Fenwick and Parsons (2000) describe various criteria that are often used to assess journal writing: overall fluency (thoroughness and variety of topics addressed), evidence of thoughtful reflection exploring various required issues or readings in the course, evidence of connection making (perhaps incorporating but moving beyond narrations of personal experience), evidence of growth (perhaps incorporating earlier responsive suggestions), and evidence of critical thinking and questioning. Depending on the purpose and context of a learning journal, some evaluators look for responses that demonstrate close listening and deep reading and that extend beyond description and report to interpretation, analyses, and connection. Some look for reflection on significant issues and concerns, considering various perspectives and viewpoints, and revealing insightful, perceptive reading and listening. Others seek evidence of

Exhibit 4.1.   Journal Assessment: Holistic Scale

5 Thoughts and feelings are purposeful and insightful. The content is either detailed or philosophically approached. The unique voice of the learner is present and sustained. Significant risks in thought may be evident. Readers can follow the presentation easily.

4 The thoughts and feelings expressed are purposeful—either insightful but general or detailed but conventional. The expression is clear, easy to follow, and appropriate for the context.

3 Thoughts and feelings are present but not always clearly connected to the purpose for language use. Language and thinking may be very conventional and lack development. Readers can follow the writer but may need to work a bit to do so. The language is generally appropriate for the context.

2 Thoughts and feelings are not consistent or connected but are related to the purpose and context. The content and expressions do not anticipate the audience. The writer knows what is meant but does not lead the reader throughout the intended meaning.

1 The content is very confusing or even conflicting. It may be only tangentially related to its intended purpose.

INS   Sample is too brief to score.

learners' risk taking, growth in insight, and stretching into complexities and patterns among issues. These are sophisticated requirements, demanding diligent commentary and even examples from evaluators throughout the journal writing period. Exhibit 4.2 is a sample rating scale that might be adapted to generate a grade applying some of these criteria.

Even when a summative grade is assigned to journal writing, an evaluator should always provide some response in dialogue. For example, evaluators can share personal thoughts that occurred in reading or comment on themes appearing throughout the journal writing. They can point out areas of growth they perceive or areas the writer might be encouraged to explore further. Above all, they must keep uppermost the honoring of the writer's process and intent, the nature of "first-draft" voice, and their role as facilitators in dialogue.

Partial Assessment. Where time limitations or the personal nature of the journal writing prohibit the reading of the whole text by an evaluator, the journal writer might select and submit a few passages for assessment. In this way the learner controls disclosure and vulnerability of personal writing. Alternatively, the journal writer may prepare and submit a few reflective pages summarizing the journal or its process for assessment. The summary might note themes appearing throughout the journal, as well as turning points and critical incidents in their development. The summary might also

Exhibit 4.2.   Sample Rating Scale for Evaluating Journals

Name_____

Evaluation Period_____

| 1 = Dependent | 2 = Limited | 3 = Adequate |
| 4 = Competent | 5 = Proficient | 6 = Superior |

| Criteria | Rating | Comments |

Responses are complete.

Responses extend beyond description and report to interpret, analyze, connect.

Responses demonstrate close listening and deep reading.

Responses link personal experience and other resources with the course material.

Responses demonstrate persistence to follow an idea.

Responses reflect on significant issues and concerns.

Responses consider various perspectives and viewpoints.

Questions reveal insightful, perceptive reading and listening.

Responses demonstrate ability to compare and evaluate.

Responses build on previous entries.

Responses show growth in insight, risk, appreciation of issue complexity, and understanding of patterns.

Journal writer's comments:

present a critical reflection, analyzing the writer's own assumptions, inferences, and beliefs as evident in the journal. Writers might choose parts of the journal writing to quote (or not) in this summary. Learners who have completed this sort of summary often remark that this synthesizing process is almost as valuable as the journal writing itself.

Self-Response. Journal writers may want to review and respond to their own journals periodically or at the conclusion of a learning period. Rereading one's own reflective outpourings is a rather complex experience. Much of the writing may seem to be self-indulgent, overly sentimental, or pure junk depending on one's mood or frame of mind at the time of rereading. Encourage learners to honor their own writing, perhaps treating it as different voices or even different selves springing freely onto the page, all trusting the reader to enjoy what is written as a raw first draft. A focus is sometimes helpful for self-response. For example, learners can try jotting notes while rereading, asking themselves, for example: "Which reflections draw my attention most on this day?" "What do I feel today as I reread?" Journal writers might try free-writing a piece after rereading their reflections, noting themes and questions that recur, connections that seem interesting, or parts where they detect particular confusion or clarity. They might also write more generally on what they learned about themselves as they reread or about the process of journal writing.

Conclusion

When we, as responders, insert ourselves into the intensely personal process of journal writing, we must be absolutely clear about our purposes and rationale, as well as our potentially repressive influence. We need to be thoughtful about the mode and role of response that we adopt at different times in the process. Flexibility is essential: balancing freedom and direction, adjusting our responses to the journal writer's needs, and checking how our responses are understood or misunderstood. We must be caring and intuitive, attending to the writer's own direction. But we need to care for our own needs too; it is easy to become overwhelmed by the sheer volume of text to read. We are more likely to truly enjoy the startling fresh insights and vivid, bold writing that journals so often yield if we limit the amount we read and the time we spend at one sitting.

Although journal writing has been used extensively in adult education and work settings, it has not always been introduced with purpose, models, helpful response, or care and sensitivity for the writer. It is not surprising that some learners have become cynical or cautious about journal writing. Our opportunity as responders is to help create a transformative journal writing experience. We can start by entering the process as gentle others interested in meaningful dialogue, offering encouraging and substantive responses, and committing ourselves to the importance of journaling in learning.

References

Berthoff, A. "Dialectical Notebooks and the Audit of Meaning." In T. Fulwiler (ed.), *The Journal Book.* Portsmouth, N.H.: Boynton/Cook, 1987.

Berthoff, A. "Reclaiming the Active Mind." *College English,* 1999, *61,* 671–680.

Elbow, P. *Writing with Power.* New York: Oxford University Press, 1981.

Fenwick, T., and Parsons, J. *The Art of Evaluation: A Handbook for Educators and Trainers.* Toronto: Thompson Educational Publishers, 2000.

Foucault, M. *Power/Knowledge: Selected Interviews and Other Writings, 1972–1977.* (C. Gordon, ed. and trans.). Brighton, England: Harvester Press, 1980.

Kirby, D., and Liner, T., with Vinz, R. *Inside Out: Developmental Strategies for Teaching Writing.* (2nd ed.) Portsmouth, N.H.: Heinemann, 1988.

Newman, J. *Interwoven Conversations.* Portsmouth, N.H.: Heinemann, 1991.

Usher, R., and Edwards, R. "Confessing All? A 'Postmodern' Guide to the Guidance and Counseling of Adult Learners." *Studies in the Education of Adults,* 1995, 27, 9–23.

Tara J. Fenwick is an assistant professor of adult education at the University of Alberta, specializing in workplace learning and continuing education.

5

The use of journals in university nursing education, as well as their role in continuing professional development for nurses and other health professionals working in clinical settings, are the focus of this chapter.

Journal Writing in Health Education

Angela J. Gillis

Journal writing is both a process and a product. As a product, journals are personally written accounts that promote the expression of perspectives, ideas, and feelings. They are one means of enabling nurses and others to address challenging educational and practice-based issues and simultaneously getting in touch with the depth, complexity, sensitivity, and even humor experienced as they journey through their educational experience. A journal in the health education context is more than and different from a diary (a daily record of personal experiences and observations) or a log (a structured, factual account of events maintained on a prescribed basis over a period of time). A journal combines the objective data of a log with the personal expressions of a diary and becomes a tool for personal growth and development.

The unique and discriminating characteristic of journal as product is its ability to create an interactive dialogue between the writer of the journal and the reader. This dynamic dimension distinguishes the journal from other forms of communication that are primarily descriptive in nature. Through journals, the writer and the reader create a personal exchange in which each tries to make meaning out of the lived experience of the learning situation (Holmes, 1997).

As a process, journaling is a popular method of promoting exploration and facilitating reflection on learning and new experiences within the context in which the learning unfolds. In health education in general, and nursing education in particular, journals are useful in locating the personal in the fast-paced health care environments that are increasingly dominated by technology and impersonal procedures against a backdrop of market forces and competition (Koch, 1998). This context makes it difficult for learners to maintain a sense of connection to their clients, creates a sense of emotional impoverishment in learners, and distances them from the art of their profession. Journal writing is a useful tool to help learners deal with such disparaging experiences.

The primary purpose of journal writing in health education is to provide an opportunity for learners to describe, interpret, and analyze their learning experiences and perspectives (Bunkers, 2000). The act of reflectively writing about one's learning contributes to the development of higher-level conceptual skills by enhancing understanding. To accomplish this purpose, three integral skill sets are required: introspection, reflection, and dialogue. These skills, taken together, propel journaling far beyond mere documentation to a "personal, mutual, phenomenological process based on dialogue in which the writer and reader try to discover and make sense of the lived experience of clinical nursing" (Holmes, 1997, p. 489). I am aware of how impossible it is for learners in many health care settings to explore and integrate their ideas and new learning into practice situations. Much of what occurs in the practice environment goes unspoken, unquestioned, and unchallenged. Journaling provides an opportunity for learners to speak and listen to the voice of practice.

Journal Writing Skills

The primary skills in journal writing are introspection, reflection, and dialogue. The honing of these skills is important for health professionals because they influence every element of health care practice. These skills help practitioners to recognize patterns in their world and communicate these patterns to themselves and others to further their understanding of the health care world.

Introspection. Introspection is the ability to focus inward and examine assumptions and prejudices. It is a means for learners to get in touch with their personal voice through quiet thought, inner searching, and time spent examining their actions, beliefs, attitudes, and values. Out of this inner thought process comes new knowledge.

Introspection is an essential skill for health professionals who wish to engage in critical thinking and detailed examination of thoughts and ideas. Journals can be used to write down new ideas and different ways of looking at the world that emerge during the quiet introspection. Journals become the original site for description of a new idea that the writer comes to own personally.

Reflection. Reflection is the skill of making our thoughts and ideas visible through descriptions that allow us to recreate experiences. It comes from the verb *reflectere*, which means to bend or turn backward. Through reflection, we take our assumptions and prejudices, identified in the introspection stage, and examine how they relate to our current and past clinical experiences. The learner begins to create authentic knowledge.

By combining introspection and reflection skills, learners come to see inconsistencies in the world of health care practice. From these inconsistencies emerge new ways of viewing the world as the learners reflect on the dissonance created during the reflective process. Both reflection and introspection require risk-taking behavior, creative thinking, independent action, and enhanced self-awareness in order to express the authentic voice of the learner in the journal entries.

Dialogue. The skill of dialogue represents an open and expansive exchange of ideas and thoughts expressed through the one-to-one exchange between the writer and the reader of the journal. Through dialogue, the learner gives expression to the new knowledge that emerges from the processes of introspection and reflection. Dialogue is important to health professionals as learners because it enables them to communicate tangibly to the reader their abstract thought processes that lead to emerging patterns, recognition of fallacies or limitations in their thinking, and eventually new knowledge and ideas about the health care world. The reader responds to the learner's comments and invites the learner to continue to expand her or his thinking and learning relating to the issue or experience. The reader may be anyone the learner chooses to share the journal with: a teacher, nursing professor, fellow student, or peer. (In Chapter Four, Fenwick goes into detail on the subject of responding to journals in a learning process.)

The skill of dialogue is closely fused with the skills of reflection and introspection. The dialogue created through written journal entries fixes thoughts on paper and externalizes for the reader and the writer what had been internal until this point. Written dialogue serves to distance us from the closeness of a lived experience. As the writer reads the written entry, the writer's objectified thinking stares back at her or him, prompting a recursive pattern of reflection and further introspection (Van Manen, 1990; Chinn, 1994). As Hancock (1999) notes, the act of writing helps to clarify issues, focuses our attention, and affirms our ideas. The interrelationship of writing, reflection, and introspection is powerful.

Three-Step Method of Journaling

A popular teaching-learning strategy used in university nursing programs where I teach is the three-step method of journaling. This experiential method combines the skills of reflection and introspection with journal writing and peer group discussion. In our nursing programs, this strategy has proven useful in preparing graduates who are capable of critical analysis, self-reflection, self-evaluation, enhanced self-awareness, and self-directed learning. These are important outcomes of the educational process, particularly in a health care environment that calls for increasing autonomy and accountability from its practitioners.

The three-step method is taught to students in the second year of our nursing program, as they initiate community-based clinical placements. Once students learn the process, they can transfer it to any of the community- or institutional-based clinical placements in subsequent years of the program. My colleagues and I have adapted this experiential learning strategy from the Riley-Doucet and Wilson (1997) proposed model.

At an initial clinical conference, students are introduced to the idea of journaling by a member of the faculty. Clarifying the process roles of faculty members, students, and fellow learners often requires considerable elaboration as each player takes on roles that are often different from their traditional functions. For example, faculty members assume new roles as mentors, risk takers, and true partners in the learning process. The role of students is to share with the faculty member and other learners their learning needs and their self-directed plans for meeting their needs and evaluating their learning outcomes. Peers take on the role of support persons and facilitators.

Once everyone clearly understands the roles, examples of journaling entries are provided (see Exhibit 5.1), and written guidelines for preparing journals are discussed. Several conference sessions are spent exploring the use of guidelines and supporting students in their experimentation with this process.

When clinical practice sessions begin, students meet at the end of each clinical day or clinical week, depending on the setting, to discuss significant events arising from the clinical experience. Students use this clinical conference as an opportunity to talk about their journal entries, if they so wish, and receive feedback from the other players. Sharing of the journal with the group is a student's choice. The journal is considered the property of the student and, hence, the student is not required to share it with the group; nevertheless, it must be shared with a faculty member. Most students, however, share their journal entries with the other students and benefit from the dialogue that results.

Step 1: Critical Appraisal of Reflective Practice. A critical analysis of the clinical practice experience represents the first step of the journal process for students in our bachelor of science in nursing program. This requires a reflective examination of their practice experience. Such reflection is important to the experiential approach of nursing education and adult education. It is also important to an understanding of one's personal learning processes. As Paul (1992) notes, this reflection is "the art of thinking about your thinking while you are thinking in order to make your thinking better, more clear, more accurate or more defensible" (p. 37). To assist nursing students in appraising their practice critically, they are provided with Hancock's list of characteristic points (1999, p. 38) that they can use for the internal examination of their clinical learning experiences. Their reflections should:

Exhibit 5.1.   Example of a Journal Entry

- Be based in their practice experiences
- Help turn their clinical experiences into new learning opportunities
- Be capable of raising their self-awareness
- Develop their intellectual skills
- Liberate students from traditional, conventional ways of thinking
- Be both an adult and experiential learning technique
- Enhance their personal and professional learning
- Empower them and assist in the development of nursing knowledge

At this step students are encouraged to write what they assess to be important and critical to their learning. The format includes answering three questions about the nursing practice experience: What? So what? and Now what? Emphasis is placed on student growth and enhanced self-awareness, critical reflection, and introspection. Exhibit 5.1 illustrates selected quotations from a student's journal as she describes her learning experiences and makes meaning from the experience.

Step 2: Peer Group Discussion. The second step in this recursive learning process is the opportunity to raise questions, concerns, and areas of dissonance that emerge from the introspection and self-reflection about the clinical events. Through clinical conferences, students have a chance to engage in dialogue with each other and with the assigned faculty member about their reflections, experiences, and new learning. The faculty member's role in this situation is to help students articulate their concerns, ideas, and emotions, as well as to assist the student in seeing the essential linkages among theory, practice, and research that emerge from the students' descriptions of their clinical situations. This step is critically important because it makes practice visible to the student. The faculty member strives to create a supportive learning environment where collaboration, rather than competition, is evident in group discussion.

The role of peers in this step is to provide feedback that helps the student to grow professionally. Peers who are in the same or similar learning situations are helpful because they know the context within which the learning is occurring. Peer feedback in this venue merely reflects another person's assessment at the time. Peer feedback is neither right nor wrong. The student decides whether to accept the feedback offered by peers and apply it constructively to improve his or her practice.

Step 3: Self-Awareness to Self-Evaluation. Following the clinical conference, students independently complete the third step of this process by documenting additional learning outcomes that emerged from the peer group discussions during the clinical conference. At this point, students document new insights that emerged from the group discussions, as well as changes they noted within themselves. Usually, I find that the clinical conference experience positively influences the introspection and reflective writing process by providing peer feedback and an opportunity to articulate what has happened to the learner as a result of introspection, reflection, and peer debriefing and discussion. Through the process of writing, analyzing, reflecting, and rewriting, nursing students come to see themselves in the center of the learning process. If they so choose, students are able to use their journal entries to show progress in meeting their learning needs. This fact enhances their sense of empowerment and personalizes the learning experience for them.

Practical Guidelines for Writing Journal Entries

At the introductory conference on the use of journals, a faculty member provides students with some written guidelines to assist them in preparing their journal entries. Experience has made me aware that it is best not to overwhelm students with too many specific directions for journal entries. Rather, journal writing should be a creative and liberating process that gives students permission to construct knowledge from their own feelings, thoughts, ideas, and observations. The following guidelines have proven useful for students embarking on the journaling process:

- Establish a clear statement of purpose for the use of journaling in your clinical learning experience that is mutually agreed on by you, the writer, and the reader.
- Begin the use of journal entries with your first clinical experience.
- Make regular journal entries so that the progress of your learning can be traced.
- Immediacy should be a guiding principle in your journaling. Record entries either concurrently with the learning experience or as soon as possible after completion of your clinical experience.
- A spiral notebook is the most useful tool to keep together a progressive record of your learning.
- Use a double-entry format with the left column reserved for descriptive narrative and the right column designated for reflection and critical analysis. The left column should contain a narrative of the meaningful events and behaviors that transpired during the clinical experience in chronological order. The right column should consist of an analysis of the critical thinking situations that resulted from your experience. Here you may record (1) your thoughts, ideas, feelings, emotions, and concerns about the clinical experience, (2) new learning, questions, and insights gained from the process of reflection and introspection about the clinical experience, (3) a critique of the learning situation, and (4) suggestions for future learning implications in the clinical context.
- Maintain a section on personal learning objectives that you evaluate on a regular basis. Try using the following questions to guide your reflection on personal learning achievements:

What have I learned from this experience?
How have I changed as a result of this learning?
Has my involvement in this experience changed the way I practice nursing?
How might my past experiences be helpful in this new situation?
How do I feel about this experience?
How do you know you have learned?

- Keep a section to record new questions or challenges that have emerged for you as a result of the clinical experience and the process of journal writing.

Students are not strictly required to follow these guidelines, although most find it helpful to do so. If students find another format more effective in promoting critical reflection and description, they are requested to discuss their thoughts with the faculty member responsible for the clinical learning experience and together reach a decision as to how the critical analysis and reflection will be recorded. To date, I have found this flexible approach has worked well in the nursing program where I teach.

Journaling as a Tool for Continuing Competence

Journaling has been accepted internationally as a valued learning tool in continuing-competence programs in countries such as Canada, Australia, the United States, and the United Kingdom. *Continuing competence* is defined as the promotion of good practice through Continuous Quality Improvement. As health care professionals, nurses have a responsibility to maintain their competence to practice according to preestablished standards of care determined by their professional associations. Continuing-competence programs provide nurses with the opportunity to step back, reflect on their practice, and decide what steps they wish to take to improve their nursing practice (Registered Nurses Association of Nova Scotia, 1999). Journaling is an effective tool to help nurses who have completed a self-assessment of their practice and developed a learning plan based on the self-assessment to reflect on and systematically evaluate the impact of their learning on their practice.

The primary reasons that nurses in continuing-competence programs maintain a journal are to address the gap between theory and practice and to provide a record of the learning that emerges from their reflection about their practice. The journal itself is effective as a means of continuing education that places control of learning with the individual nurse. The process of reflective journaling moves the experienced nurse from a teacher-dependent learning mode to a student-centered one, whereby the student is responsible for identifying, exploring, and fulfilling their learning needs (Jasper, 1999). Hence, through journaling, nurses may be motivated to be proactive and responsive to new learning and challenges.

As experienced nurses reflect on their practice and write entries in their journals, they come to identify strengths and limitations in the way they practice nursing. They recognize that they learn from their experiences and come to observe patterns of behavior over time. This process is always more significant in identifying strengths and limitations than isolated events such as workshops. Adjustments may be required in the journal writing process for new nurses versus experienced nurses, who have developed expertise in analyzing their practice. Often, seasoned nurses let their writing flow uncensored and develop their own style. They may leave space in their journals to go back and add reflections about a situation that occurred some time after the initial recording of a situation. I have found that a flexible approach enables experienced nurses to explore strengths in practice skill areas and identify areas for further growth. A more rigid adherence to rules or guidelines for reflective journaling leads the experienced nurses to focus on the exercise itself rather than on the learning environment of their practice; consequently, it inhibits exploration and defeats the purpose of journaling in continuing-competence programs. At this point in a nurse's career, journaling should deepen the level of reflection and analysis of practice rather than constrain thoughts by focusing too strictly on guidelines for writing. This approach is in contrast to that used with the new nurse who, like many other nursing students, may first have to learn the skills of reflective writing before accepting writing as a learning strategy with merit of its own.

One caution when working with nurses in continuing-competence programs is the need to focus on explicit outcomes of reflective journaling. If outcomes are not stressed, nurses may question the value of the reflection and the time spent doing it. Outcomes should always include highlights of the new learning (personal and professional) that have emerged from the reflection and a discussion of how this learning will affect and change the practice of the nurse. As one registered nurse explained, "I have learned a lot about nursing from this process, which I expected to, but, surprisingly, I have learned more about myself than I thought possible. It is like a voyage of self-discovery and sometimes it is really threatening. This new self-awareness is what really makes a difference in the way I now approach nursing. I never would have believed this at the outset."

Outcomes of Journaling

Many outcomes result from journaling as part of a planned approach to continuing competence for registered nurses. These should be explicitly explained to nurses who are embarking on this journey. Some of these outcomes include:

- The development of skills in critical thinking, reflection, self-awareness, and self-confidence
- New theoretical and practical learning that can lead to improved care
- Enhanced progress, growth, and accountability as a professional
- Tangible commitment to remain current in a practice area

- Uncovering knowledge already possessed but used without awareness
- Monitoring knowledge and skill development over time
- A base for understanding theory, a means to assess its relevancy to practice, and an understanding of when and how to adapt it to fit the realities of practice

As experienced nurses participate in continuing-competence programs, they will be eager to see tangible results from their participation. The application of the new learning that has emerged from their journaling experience must now be integrated with their previous nursing knowledge. This is an exciting and dynamic challenge to see practice transformed through reflection and introspection. As I see it, even experienced nurses need the support of their colleagues and peers to continue to seize opportunities for professional growth. Participation in continuing-competence programs should develop nurses' self-esteem and self-awareness and place them in the best possible position to do this.

Implications and Future Trends in Journaling

The use of journals in nursing education, health education, and practice settings is creating a new educational paradigm where theoretical and practical knowledge join to reinforce learning and contribute to the development of professionals who are capable of critical thinking. A significant implication of journals is their ability to identify biases inherent in the beliefs and value systems of students and professionals. With these opportunities to make their epistemological assumptions explicit, students can examine their values and write about their experiences from a new perspective.

It appears certain that the use of reflective journals by health professional students and practitioners will continue to grow in the future. Journals will remain an important form of continuing education and become integral to most continuing-competency programs. They are a cost-effective, highly portable, low-technology option with unlimited usefulness. They can be used with all groups of health professionals across a wide range of institutional and community-based services to improve practice, stimulate personal and professional growth of the practitioner, and help narrow the theory-practice gap that exists in health care.

The use of reflective journals appears to be fully endorsed internationally by nurse educators and others. The literature provides rich and informative accounts of the use of journals in nursing education, midwifery, community health, home care, continuing education, and spirituality and palliative care programs. While this fact is encouraging for those who are striving to create humanistic learning environments for health professionals, there is some evidence that the reflective practice movement may be threatened by the rationalization of both clinical and theoretical education in universities and other settings. It will be important to continue to monitor the outcomes of reflective practice and to encourage process and outcome evaluations of its effectiveness.

As we strive for excellence in professional education, the role of teachers and faculty in supporting and guiding students to become reflective practitioners cannot be overemphasized. Appropriate feedback, monitoring, and encouragement are critical to preparing practitioners who can ask probing questions of themselves and others and analyze information appropriately to inform practice. As Lyons (1999) notes, "If knowledge is power, then knowledge about who we are and how we practise is even more powerful" (p. 34). The journey of discovery rather than the destination is the key process to unleashing this power within us.

References

Bunkers, S. S. "Growing Story: A Teaching-Learning Process." *Nursing Science Quarterly,* 2000, *13,* 24–30.

Chinn, P. *Advances in Methods of Inquiry for Nursing.* Gaithersburg, Md.: Aspen, 1994.

Hancock, P. "Reflective Practice—Using a Learning Journal." *Nursing Standard,* 1999, *13,* 37–40.

Holmes, V. "Grading Journals in Clinical Practice: A Delicate Issue." *Journal of Nursing Education,* 1997, *36,* 489–491.

Jasper, M. "Nurses' Perceptions of the Value of Written Reflection." *Nurse Education Today,* 1999, *19,* 452–463.

Koch, T. "Story Telling: Is It Really Research?" *Journal of Advanced Nursing,* 1998, *28,* 1182–1190.

Lyons, J. "Reflective Education for Professional Practice: Discovering Knowledge from Experience." *Nurse Education Today,* 1999, *19,* 29–34.

Paul, R. "Critical Thinking: What, Why, and How." In C. Barns (ed.), *Critical Thinking: An Educational Imperative.* San Francisco: Jossey-Bass, 1992.

Registered Nurses Association of Nova Scotia. *Building Your Profile.* Halifax, Nova Scotia, Canada: Registered Nurses Association of Nova Scotia, 1999.

Riley-Doucet, C., and Wilson, S. "A Three-Step Method of Self-Reflection Using Reflective Journal Writing." *Journal of Advanced Nursing,* 1997, *25,* 964–968.

Van Manen, M. *Researching Lived Experience.* London, Ontario, Canada: University of Western Ontario, 1990.

Angela J. Gillis is professor and chair of the Department of Nursing at Saint Francis Xavier University, Antigonish, Nova Scotia.

Women's journals are a unique treasure that provide a glimpse into the lives of individuals whose voices otherwise would not have been heard. Journals continue to be a source of inspiration and revelation for the women who write them and those who read them.

Women, Journal Writing, and the Reflective Process

Elizabeth A. Peterson, Ann M. Jones

Women's journals provide a glimpse into the lives of women and into a history that had no space for women's voices. Journals have helped raise the consciousness of those women who believed the myths that led to their own self-degradation. By chronicling their suffering and oppression, many women were able to find solace and create a safe space for themselves. In this sense, journal writing was a way for women to work through their problems, address concerns, and evaluate their growth without fear of outside judgment or reprisal. Gilligan (1982) believes that women innately give up a sense of self and voice in order to preserve relationships. Women have a sense of interrelationship that men do not have. They define their identity through relationships of intimacy and care, but the second that they do this, they create a dependency that leads to the loss of voice.

Journals play an important role in women's lives by helping them regain their voice. Journals have enabled women to reflect on the past, present, and future and have helped them envision new or expanded possibilities. As such, journals can enhance the learning experience. Adult education relies on practitioners and students who can engage in dreaming, visioning, and reflection. Creating room for journal writing becomes an important component of any adult education program.

Women and Journals

All types of individuals use journals as a form of leisurely expression, a vehicle for reflection, and a means of recording daily events. In a sense, anyone can write a journal. The question is, Are women unique in their use and approach to journal writing?

New Directions for Adult and Continuing Education, no. 90, Summer 2001
© John Wiley & Sons, Inc.

Why Do Women Use Journals? As we see it, women's journals have provided readers a window into the world through a woman's eyes. Because history has been written primarily through a male perspective, most texts have focused on events where men have played a significant role. Women's journals and diaries have often provided the only account of a life or world lived differently. We have learned about the atrocities of the Holocaust through history books, but the diary of a young girl, Anne Frank (1967), provides a name and a face that we will always associate with this dark era. We know the reality of slavery in the United States, but it is through the writings of slave women that we know the true harshness and pain it caused as families were torn apart.

Women's use of journals is unique in that it connects so well with what we now know about women's ways of knowing. The writings of Belenky, Clinchy, Goldberger, and Tarule (1986) and Hart (1985) have addressed the characteristics of women's learning patterns. According to *Women's Ways of Knowing* (Belenky, Clinchy, Goldberger, and Tarule, 1986), women can progress through several stages of development: listening to the voices of others, listening to the inner voice, searching for self, listening to the voice of reason, and integrating the different voices. Journal writing can provide a means for women to move from a position of dependence, relying only on the knowledge that they receive from others (received knowledge), to the point where they listen to and trust their inner voice (subjective knowledge). When women begin to listen to their inner voice, they find their "inner source of strength" (p. 54).

Women's loss of self occurs in many ways without their full knowledge or awareness. Hart (1985) emphasizes the need for women to engage in consciousness-raising activities that move beyond merely supplying "factual information that has been suppressed" to those that challenge the years of "socialization in the form of well-entrenched habits or perception and experience" (p. 133). Regaining the sense of self requires conscious work and attention to personal needs. This is an active process, and journal writing can help. The use of a journal to "write the truth" can be an aid to marginalized women, who often find themselves sifting through "speech and action which are guided by motives that remain opaque and impenetrable" (Hart, 1985, p. 128).

Estes (1992) contends that the process of gaining voice is far more instinctual and an expression of a woman's own creativity: "Eventually every woman away from her soul-home tires. This is as it should be. Then she seeks her skin again in order to revive her sense of self and soul, in order to restore her deep-eyed and oceanic knowing. This great cycle of going and returning, going and returning, is reflexive within the instinctual nature of women and is innate to all women for all their lives" (p. 265).

Journal writing, according to this view, is just one form of women's expression as they instinctively seek their inner being. Although women often find other outlets for their creativity (music, dance, gardening), journaling is unique in that it makes apparent the connection among life events, ideas, emotions, and the language used to express all three. Journals encourage reflection by forcing the writer to recreate events and emotion mentally.

As part of the creative process, Daniell (1997) encourages students to write about themselves, the "I," through fantasy sharing and play, because "our fantasies are the truest parts of ourselves" (p. 6). Creative journal writing can help women to connect to the "dear self" or the deepest part of self, according to Capacchione (1989). She believes that creative journals can be used to enhance the power of intuition, a trait often credited to women. Intuition often has been devalued in an absolutist world that relies heavily on science and fact. Women learn to silence their intuition and therefore do not verbalize their hunches. Because intuition is an essential part of the creative process, journals can be used to sustain this form of subjective knowing and to enhance creativity.

How Do Women Use Journals? Regardless of the reasons that women journal, either to give voice to their lives that might otherwise remain unacknowledged or as a means of exploring their intuitions, fantasies, and dreams, the fact remains that women have long used journals. Journals have provided the means for women to record their life stories and critical events, to solve problems, and for personal discovery and self-awareness. They have helped readers trace the historical record of how cultural and social events have affected the lives of women. Readers can better understand women's struggle for a place in society. We can see areas where progress has been made, and we can also recognize that some things have not changed.

Many examples exist of how women have used journals to record important events in their lives and the feelings and emotions associated with these events. Slave women used journals and letters to record the birth and loss of their children and other loved ones and to recount the bitter experiences as property of uncaring masters. The diaries of women who have been at the forefront of many social movements have proved to be critical for researchers in understanding the progression of social change. Journals help women to find a collective source of inspiration. We believe women today can connect with their foremothers and find that they are not alone. Women of the past struggled with the same issues we face today, and they often found solutions.

Women's Journals and Adult Education

Educators have recognized that journaling can be effectively used to develop critical and creative thinking skills. For women, particularly women from marginalized groups, the journal can be a mechanism for allowing their voices to be heard for the first time. bell hooks (1994) describes how she adjusted her pedagogical strategies to enable a group of writers to "affirm their presence and right to speak": "I assign students to write an autobiographical paragraph about an early racial memory. Each person reads that paragraph aloud to the class. Our collective listening to one another affirms the value and uniqueness of each voice. This exercise highlights experience without privileging the voices of students from any particular group" (p. 84).

We have found that for women who have grown accustomed to a place or station in life, the journal can be a tool that can be used to help them move beyond the status quo. Cell (1984) believes that each person has a story to tell. As we write about the events that carry a special meaning for us, we may "grasp a fuller meaning of these events and in the situations in which we undergo them" (p. 221). This writing elevates the event or situation from being a mere occurrence to being an opportunity for learning and growth.

Using a journal to enhance the learning process is not always easy for either the instructor or the student, especially female students. The traditional educational model has not always prepared women to explore deeply the issues emanating from both the material and the educational process or to analyze their own feelings and responses to new material. Nor have instructors been prepared to teach students how to do this. Therefore, the journal writing process is often perceived to be tedious at best and often downright unnecessary and even trivial. Women when asked to keep a journal for the first time may not understand the purpose or process. Instructors who require students to keep a journal may find that they are frustrated because they do not get from students "what they want," but at the same time they may find that they cannot articulate what they want in a student's journal. The instructor bears some responsibility for helping students to understand the importance of the journal and in assisting them in the process by guiding them in a direction that will result in a positive learning experience. Therefore, instructors should always give considerable thought to what is expected in the journal and what the student may gain from writing a journal. They should never assign a journal if there is no real purpose for keeping it. When it is used for the purpose of instruction, the students should clearly know the difference between a journal and a diary, although for women sometimes the distinction may be blurred.

Barriers to Journal Writing

For women, the barriers to journal writing mimic the barriers adults face as participants in adult education. The barriers tend to fall into three categories: attitudinal, situational, and institutional barriers.

Attitudinal Barriers. Attitudinal barriers include self-doubt, lack of trust in the process, and fear of exposure. Research has shown that the experiences of girls and boys in the classroom can be very different (American Association of University Women, 1992). Although some studies have refuted the severity of gender bias in the schools (Kramer, 1992), most agree that girls' (particularly low-income girls') self-esteem as learners tends to decline over all schooling. Cohen (1997) describes a student who felt that as a learner she was inadequate and that her feelings and thoughts were not important enough to be considered in a serious classroom experience. When asked how she learned this attitude, she could recall the situation with clarity: her teacher in the third grade told she was stupid. Belenky and others (1986) describe how women are often unaware of their own intelligence. Out of fear of reprisal, these women learn to be silent.

Other difficulties arise when gender and class issues are apparent in the classroom. No matter how hard the instructor tries to eliminate it, there is a power relationship between teacher and student, and it can be exacerbated when there are differences in race and class. hooks (1994) points out the class bias inherent in the whole educational process. Class bias exists because our educational system is based on middle-class values that silence other value systems. According to hooks, "Silencing enforced by bourgeois values is sanctioned in the classroom by everyone" (p. 180).

Black women may feel highly uncomfortable writing about their personal experiences and reflections if the instructor is white, and women in general may not be as inclined to delve deeply into their feelings if the instructor is a man. Brookfield (1995) cautions educators to be aware of the fact that although journal use is popular, it can be misused: "Journal instructions that to teachers seem to embody a respectful acknowledgment of the importance of students' articulated experiences can be perceived by the students as a tool of control as repressive as the most rigid closed-book examinations. Students come to see journals as mandated disclosures focused on eliciting the right kinds of revelations" (p. 100).

Situational Barriers. Situational barriers refer to particular circumstances that can impede participation in an activity or event. When a group of female graduate students were asked what barriers prevented them from regular journal writing, by far their most frequent response was "time." One woman wrote, "The main barrier to keeping a journal regularly was time. I usually wanted to write at the end of the day and found that many times I was tired. I would put off the writing and before you know it I had not written in months." These women all worked during the day and went to school in the evenings. Although they recognized the benefit of regular journal writing (one woman stated, "I miss journaling when I'm not doing it"), they found it hard to find enough quiet, uninterrupted time to write. The women questioned had devised a number of strategies to eliminate this barrier. One student kept the journal by her bed, and the last thing she did at night was to write in it. Others found it easier to begin the day by writing in their journal.

Situational barriers such as lack of time are often exacerbated by self-doubt and fear of discovery. One woman stated that although time was her biggest barrier to journal writing, she also felt a bit uncomfortable with the thought of someone else finding and reading her journal after her death.

Another student said, "Journals are not something you can share with many people if you are honest in them." Because many women fear that one day their journals might be read by unintended readers, they spend a great deal of their writing time carefully selecting words and analyzing their entries, and then removing thoughts or images that they feel might come back to haunt them. The process of writing and rewriting adds to their sense that there is not enough time to write.

Poor writing skills can be another barrier to successful journal writing. Although the content is always more important than the mechanics, women who do not write well have more difficulty in writing. One student lamented that "she always had trouble writing." She did not feel that she wrote exactly what she wanted to say and therefore disliked being required to keep a journal.

Institutional Barriers. Although individual educators may recognize the value of student journals, more traditional educators have been slow to accept this approach. Teachers and students who are products of what Freire (1970) calls the "banking model" of education find it difficult to participate in alternative pedagogical methods. Cohen (1997) describes how the system damages learners' natural abilities and calls into question their intelligence. The teacher is the authority. Students who are successful in the traditional model learn to reject the knowledge that comes from their own experiences.

Journals present a problem for instructors who do not know how to evaluate them. In traditional environments, educators rely on seemingly objective measures of ability and progress and feel uncomfortable evaluating material that they consider too subjective and open to individual interpretation. (In Chapter Four, Fenwick explains how these problems can be overcome.)

Examples of Women's Journal Writing

Although it may be difficult to initiate journal writing activities, the process nevertheless can be enriching for both the student and the instructor. The journal gives the student and the instructor a mechanism for direct and personal communication in a way that would be impossible in the classroom setting. The following entry is from a student who initially did not want to write a journal. After taking several courses where she was required to keep a journal, she now recognizes the value of daily reflection and journal writing, particularly when confronted with new material and ideas:

> I think the most important thing that I learned was to see and treat each person as an individual. People from the same family are different, so it goes for race, nationality, gender, religion, sexual orientation, and whatever other label we want to associate with them. I want to be treated like J.—not some overweight, white, middle-aged woman. I know this is what people who don't

know me see when they look at me. But give me a chance to interact and you will find someone very different within. I learned this is true for everyone.

This student was taking a course and was often responding to material that was challenging or disturbing to her. She used her journal to "get things off her chest." As the instructor, I responded to her many questions about the new information, often giving her an alternative interpretation or suggesting other readings that could help her to find answers for herself.

Women's journals are sometimes a blend of reflection and catharsis. As they confront problems in their daily lives, it is difficult for them to compartmentalize their experiences. The next example shows how one woman used her journal to process what she was learning in class to help her deal with difficulties at work:

> [March 9, 2000] What I had always believed were barriers to participation couldn't have been farther from the truth. The more I have been reading about barriers to participation in . . . [sic] I know I need to know even more about this topic. Once you realize how wrong you have been for so long, it is exciting to think about the new knowledge and how to use it to hopefully make a difference in the future.
>
> [March 16, 2000] There are so many changes in our administration going home [sic]. I don't feel there is much job security even if you are doing the best job. I realized all the people previously in the department only stayed a year or two and moved on to private industry. . . . I don't want to leave my job, but I also want to be prepared to do something else if I need to.

How to Encourage Journal Use

There is abundant material available to instructors who wish to use journals in the classroom (Brookfield, 1995; Kerka, 1996; Walden, 1995). Kerka has specific suggestions for learners to help them overcome the fear of open-ended journals. Instructors should describe the various types of journals and their formats. They can also begin by giving specific exercises or guiding questions. Instructors should always describe how the information in the journal will be used, whether it will be shared with the class, and how it will be graded.

Self-disclosure can be a frightening proposition, especially in a classroom situation where the instructor is responsible for assigning a grade or otherwise evaluating student progress. A student's fear of disclosure can be handled in a number of ways. Brookfield (1995) chooses not to read individual journal entries but instead reads a monthly summary by students, who choose what they want to disclose. We use journal writings as an opportunity for honest exchange. In the role of instructor, we believe we can raise questions and respond to questions that the students might ask, but we never evaluate a student's analysis of an experience or praise or condemn his or her feelings. (In Chapter Four, Fenwick also explores the complexity of grading.) We believe that we have a responsibility to recognize that students may be moving out of their comfort zones and also see a responsibility to help students manage their discomfort. If a student finds herself moving into new territory, we do not just leave her there to move through it on her own. By presenting alternative ways of thinking and reasoning and pointing out gray areas in seemingly black-and-white situations, the instructor is fulfilling the role of responsible mentor and guide.

These suggestions can be combined with a multitude of other activities that can be found on the Internet and in books and articles on journaling. However, before any particular strategy will work, trust must be established. Trust in the teacher and trust in the process lay the foundation for building a relationship that encourages the free thought and honesty necessary for successful journal writing.

Although women might initially be suspicious of the process, they can and do warm up to the opportunity to speak in their own voice, listen to their internal voice, and change their meaning perspectives. In doing so, they may find new ways to live and act on their unspoken dreams, fantasies, and visions.

References

American Association of University Women. *How Schools Shortchange Girls*. Washington, D.C.: American Association of University Women, 1992.

Belenky, M., Clinchy, B., Goldberger, N., and Tarule, J. *Women's Ways of Knowing: The Development of Self, Voice, and Mind*. New York: Basic Books, 1986.

Brookfield, S. *Becoming a Critically Reflective Teacher*. San Francisco: Jossey-Bass, 1995.

Capacchione, L. *The Creative Journal: The Art of Finding Yourself*. North Hollywood, Calif.: Newcastle Publishing, 1989.

Cell, E. *Learning to Learn from Experience*. Albany, N.Y.: SUNY Press, 1984.

Cohen, L. "I Ain't So Smart, and You Ain't So Dumb: Personal Reassessment in Transformative Learning." In P. Cranton (ed.), *Transformative Learning in Action: Insights from Practice*. New Directions for Adult and Continuing Education, no. 74. San Francisco: Jossey-Bass, 1997.

Daniell, R. *The Woman Who Spilled Words All over Herself: Writing and Living the Zona Rosa Way*. Winchester, Mass.: Faber & Faber, 1997.

Estes, C. *Women Who Run with the Wolves: Myths and Stories of the Wild Woman Archetype*. New York: Ballantine Books, 1992.

Frank, A. *Anne Frank: The Diary of a Young Girl*. New York: Washington Square Press, 1967.

Freire, P. *Pedagogy of the Oppressed*. New York: Seabury, 1970.

Gilligan, C. *In a Different Voice: Psychological Theory and Women's Development*. Cambridge, Mass.: Harvard University Press, 1982.

Hart, M. "Thematization of Power, the Search for Common Interests, and Self-Reflection: Towards a Comprehensive Concept of Emancipatory Education." *International Journal of Lifelong Education*, 1985, *4*, 119–134.

hooks, b. *Teaching to Transgress: Education as the Practice of Freedom*. New York: Routledge, 1994.

Kerka, S. *Journal Writing and Adult Learning*. Columbus, Ohio: Clearinghouse on Adult, Career, and Vocational Education, 1996. (ED 399 413) [http://www.ericacve.org/docs/dig174.htm].

Kramer, R. "Are Girls Shortchanged in School?" *Commentary*, 1992, *93*, 48—49.

Walden, P. "Journal Writing: A Tool for Women Developing as Knowers." In K. Taylor and C. Marienau (eds.), *Learning Environments for Women's Adult Development: Bridges Toward Change.* New Directions for Adult and Continuing Education, no. 65. San Francisco: Jossey-Bass, 1995.

Elizabeth A. Peterson is an associate professor of adult education at the University of South Carolina.

Ann M. Jones is a training facilitator for the South Carolina Department of Corrections and an adjunct professor at the University of South Carolina.

7

Uses of journal writing in adult English as a Second Language teacher education and classroom teaching are the focus of this chapter. Examples of journal writing discussed are teacher collaborative journals, Web-based journals, and student-teacher dialogue journals.

Journal Writing in Adult ESL: Improving Practice Through Reflective Writing

Richard A. Orem

Over the past thirty years, the practice of teaching second or foreign languages has experienced dramatic shifts, influenced in large measure by philosophical debates and emerging research informing the study of learning in general and second-language acquisition in particular. I can recall vividly, as a high school freshman nearly forty years ago, my first encounter with learning a foreign language, French. My teacher was a recent college graduate and well trained in audiolingual methodology, the latest foreign language teaching approach, known for its rigid adherence to procedure, its emphasis on inductive learning of rules, and its precise mimicry of sounds by the learner in imitation of native speakers.

The pendulum of changing philosophical forces in second-language teaching has swung far and wide since 1965. We have moved from teacher-centered approaches, such as audiolingual methodology, to highly learner-centered approaches influenced by humanistic psychology with its emphasis on the whole person (Richards and Rodgers, 1986). We have seen the pendulum swing from emphasizing linguistic competence and grammar structures to emphasizing communicative competence and learning strategies (Nunan, 1990). And we have seen the pendulum swing from viewing language learning as simply learning academic subject matter to viewing language learning as a political act and a potentially transformative, even emancipatory, act (Auerbach, 1992).

Within this context of the changing world of second-language teaching, I discuss the role of journal writing as technique in the preparation of

NEW DIRECTIONS FOR ADULT AND CONTINUING EDUCATION, no. 90, Summer 2001 adult English as a Second Language (ESL) educators, as well as a teaching technique in adult ESL classrooms.

Journal Writing in ESL Teacher Preparation

The practice of teaching adults ESL has been a marginal enterprise in North American education systems. Practitioners of adult ESL have struggled to gain recognition as a legitimate field of professional practice. This profession of adult ESL is tainted by the fact that the majority of adult ESL practitioners lack sufficient preparation to be effective in their practice; those who have both experience and training, and they are in the minority, work largely as part-timers or volunteers (Crandall, 1993). In sum, we have a population of largely unprepared, marginalized, and isolated practitioners, factors that lead to high turnover and a heavy burden on local programs to provide meaningful staff development activities. Given these conditions, journal writing can be an effective tool for continuing staff development.

Gebhard and Oprandy (1999), and Richards and Lockhart (1994) advocate a program of ESL teacher development through reflective practice. An important component of reflective practice for all of these teacher educators is the teaching journal, which is a record of observations and responses to events that occur in the teaching-learning transaction. Some teachers may go so far as to audiotape or videotape their teaching. However, the meat of the journal is written observation and interpretation of the practice of teaching. The following excerpt comes from my own teaching journal of several years ago:

> Yesterday I got my student evaluations back from last semester. For the first time I received perfect scores across the board. Was I ever pleased! I knew that class was special, call it chemistry, or good vibes, I really enjoyed it, and it must have showed. But I wasn't able to enjoy the moment for very long. Last night, one of my students approached me after class and told me how much she didn't like how the class was organized! She didn't like all the group work. At first, she said she didn't feel the group was pulling their weight. The more we talked, however, it became apparent that she didn't like group work period. So I began to think about what she was bringing to the class and how she might be influenced by her own "baggage." And then it became more clear to me. First, she's much younger than any other student in this class. She doesn't have the life experience that the others are bringing to the table. Second, this is her first graduate-level class in the program. Most of the others have had at least one other class. I tried to persuade her to suspend her own judgment about the class until she's had some more time. I think she may be having some other stresses in her life as well. I definitely need to check back on her on a regular basis, maybe pair her up with one of the older students to serve as some kind of mentor. I don't want to necessar-

ily change my teaching style for the whole class because of one student. Everyone else seems to be enjoying it. I need to think through this one more carefully!

Keeping a teaching journal can be a daunting task for the practitioner. It requires adherence to a routine and the willingness for self-evaluation and reflection, thus forcing the teacher to ask difficult questions of what worked and did not work and why. In the example above, I was quick to make several assumptions about my own teaching: that what works for one class should work for another and that all students will like specific techniques, such as small-group work. I was quick to look at the group as a whole, without examining some of the individual differences that could be affected by my teaching style. By reflecting on these assumptions, I was able to come up with several possible solutions to my own problem.

Adult ESL teachers, especially part-timers, frequently experience isolation in the workplace. Some work in satellite campuses, such as church basements, libraries, or community centers. A teacher may be the only teacher present at a particular time of the day. Her or his only contact with other teachers might be an occasional staff meeting on the main campus or a social function organized by one of the teachers or the school. Staff development activities frequently focus on program management issues such as record keeping, not teaching issues. It is easy to see why there would be such a high turnover of these part-timers. For these teachers, program directors should seriously consider implementing a program of collaborative journal writing (Brock, Wong, and Yu, 1993; Dong, 1997), which requires several teachers to participate by selecting a range of topics they will write about. Topics might include specific teacher behaviors, student responses, or student-teacher interactions. Following each class, the teacher writes a personal observation that is then distributed to the others who have agreed to write. The teachers respond to each other as soon as possible. Teachers meet weekly to discuss their observations and reactions and how the journal writing experience is influencing their teaching.

With the development of interactive computer-based technology, engaging each other in Web-based discussions can offset physical isolation often felt by some teachers. WebBoard is a popular software product that enables teachers who are physically isolated to engage in extended asynchronous discussions on common topics. I recently introduced my graduate students to WebBoard for purposes of extending class discussion beyond the formal meeting time. This software product is important because the great majority of my students have full-time jobs and study part time. But in observing my graduate students' use of WebBoard as part of their class assignment, I also realized how this software could provide a forum for collaborative journal writing. As an example, in the following excerpt, two teachers share their experiences through a collaborative journal technique. One is a novice teacher who has just started her first class.

The second teacher has been teaching for six months. What is new is that they are communicating over the Internet using a WebBoard-threaded discussion format.

> [Teacher 1, Tuesday, 10 A.M.] I started my ESL teaching job last night. It was a real eye-opener. I was told that I would have 10 students. Before the class was over, I had 25 students. Needless to say, I wasn't prepared with enough books or handouts. I had a lesson planned but couldn't even get to it because another student would show up every five minutes. On top of that, I had some students who were fairly advanced in their oral skills, and some who had only arrived in the community within the last two weeks and could barely utter any English at all. I was overwhelmed! I've tried to contact the program coordinator but she hasn't returned my call yet. HELP! I know we talked about these issues in our methods class, but it really doesn't sink in until you experience it. I meet with them again tomorrow night.

> [Teacher 2, Tuesday, 4 P.M.] Welcome to the world of adult ESL! First, catch your breath and try to relax. Did you notice that the students probably weren't as upset as you? Did you have any time to do any initial language assessments? Probably not. The resource room at the center has some good materials for grouping students at the beginning of your class so that you can work individually with some students on their language assessment. Probably the program coordinator has already returned your call by now. I know she is really responsive. And don't worry! These first few days of the quarter are always the most hectic!

> [Teacher 1, Tuesday, 7 P.M.] Thanks for the encouragement. Yes, Mary returned my call this afternoon and we had a long conversation. She gave me a lot of good ideas, and she offered to come to the class to help me with the initial assessments. I feel much better now. I'll let you know how it goes after tomorrow night's class. I really need to work on being more patient. I've learned that about myself throughout this graduate program. I expect everything to work the first time. I need to expect failure, but it's hard for me to deal with it. I've also got to think more about the students' perspective. Now that I think about it, that's what we have been talking about in class for the last semester. OK, I'm feeling better now. Talk to you after tomorrow's class.

This Web-based collaborative journal enables the dialogue between these two teachers to continue without the need to be physically present and without limits of time. Reflections can be recorded at any time, day or night. In fact, these two teachers were forty miles apart while they participated in this threaded discussion. They were united only by the Internet.

A major anticipated outcome of reflective journal writing by teachers is that they not only will come to understand their own actions better, but will use journals as a way to engage in their own research into the practice of teaching (Carroll, 1994). To that end, Quigley and Kuhne (1997) advocate the use of action research by adult educators and identify the reflective journal as an important source of data in such research. Action research is a process of seeking answers to problems that have direct application to improving practice in education or any other work setting. Reflective journals help teachers to gain practice in asking questions.

Journal Writing as a Teaching Technique

Just as journal writing is gaining in popularity in teacher education and staff development programs, it is also gaining popularity as a technique in the adult ESL classroom. Its use varies greatly depending on the purposes of instruction and the training and confidence level of the classroom teacher. This discussion looks at the use of journals as a tool for teaching ESL in classrooms that can be characterized as emphasizing structural approaches, those using more communicative approaches, and those using more critical approaches in teaching ESL.

I define communicative approaches as those that stress the teaching of language for purposes of oral and written interaction, in contrast to structural approaches, which emphasize the teaching of language structure (grammar and syntax). Most adult ESL programs today advocate communicative approaches for teaching language that is used in general social and employment settings. Examples of structural approaches are commonly found in academic settings, such as preparing students to take the Test of English as a Foreign Language for college admission. Critical approaches, however, tend to view language as a means to an end, and the end is seen as empowering students, enabling them to gain some measure of control in their lives and to analyze their work and social contexts in terms of power relationships (Pennycook, 1999). Journal writing can be found in any classroom, but the goal of it varies dramatically depending on whether the focus is on language structure, language for communication, or language for empowerment.

The goal of successful second-language teaching in programs advocating a structural approach is control of the basic mechanics of language, for example, grammar and pronunciation. Journals in these classrooms are seen as opportunities to practice correct language forms. Teachers focus on error correction and can use student writing samples for feedback as to how well the students are applying the rules of grammar.

A major goal of successful second-language teaching in communicative classrooms is the effective integration of the basic communication skills in each lesson. In other words, how do you best integrate listening, speaking, reading, and writing in a way that produces meaningful language in an authentic context? Communication, not totally correct language forms, is the goal. As language educators have become more interested in communicative writing (Johnson and Roen, 1989; Leki, 1992; Raimes, 1983) within the context of more interactive classrooms, the use of dialogue journals has been quickly identified as an important technique for teaching both reading and writing. An early publication on dialogue journals in ESL classrooms provides some excellent examples of this interactive form of instruction (Peyton, 1990).

The goal of dialogue journal writing found in communicative classrooms, and largely espoused by Peyton and her colleagues (Peyton and Reed, 1990), focuses more on the constructivist (meaning-making) dimension of learning and literacy. As a technique, dialogue journal writing responds to the learner's need to communicate with others in a meaningful context. The following excerpt is taken from a dialogue journal written by a young adult who has been studying ESL for six months; it is followed by the teacher's comments. The setting is a recent visit to the local public library:

> [Student] I like the library. I want to read because I know I will learning English faster if I read. Thank you for take the class to the library. When are we going again?

> [Teacher] I'm glad you liked the library. You don't have to wait for the class to visit. You can go to the library anytime you want. You have a library card so you can use it now to check books out. What kind of books do you like?

Notice that the teacher did not point out the student's language errors. Rather, in her response, she modeled the correct forms so that the student could see them in the natural context of this dialogue.

Communicative classrooms stress purpose and audience (Why am I writing this? Who will read this?). In a typical classroom, the teacher and the curriculum often determine instructional goals, and the audience is frequently the teacher. However, more effective teachers will allow the learner to decide the purpose, and the audience will be expanded to include others, such as other students. One format for extending the potential audience in a more interactive writing program has been the use of pen pals. With the popularity and widespread use of e-mail, this medium provides opportunities for more immediate feedback by a much wider audience.

Dialogue journals in communicative classrooms are also characterized by an emphasis on writing for communication. The students are interested in not only communicating but also perfecting their skills. Teachers need to be careful not to dampen a student's enthusiasm with excessive correction. In order to avoid this problem, some teachers inform students at the beginning of the activity that student journals will be read for content alone, not for form. The term *dialogue journal* implies that there will be a conversation between writer and reader. It attempts to simulate the authentic exchange of language outside the formal classroom.

The goal of journal writing in more participatory classrooms is to empower students to write about issues of concern to them and to seek answers through the journal as how best to deal with these issues. Auerbach (1992) has written extensively on the subject of participatory approaches to teaching ESL. According to Auerbach, "The central tenet of a participatory approach is that curricula must emerge from and be responsive to the particular context of each group of participants" (p. 1). Journals are a natural source for student-generated materials in the participatory classroom. As such, teachers must be prepared to deal with some sensitive issues in the lives of their students. Many students will be reluctant to reveal these issues until a relationship of trust has been built between them and the teacher. On the one hand, they need to be assured that whatever they write will be kept confidential. On the other hand, journals can be cathartic experiences for students who will use this opportunity to talk about problems in the workplace (such as harassment and documentation), the home (such as domestic violence), and the community (such as police profiling). They may raise issues of health (such as acquired immunodeficiency syndrome and other sexually transmitted diseases) or the education of their children (such as tracking). Teachers need to be prepared to respond to these issues immediately and in confidence. (Chapters Three and Four also discuss issues of confidentiality and response.)

The following journal excerpt was written by a student in an intermediate adult ESL class who had been attending regularly until the previous week. The teacher and the student had developed a personal relationship over the previous year. The teacher had actively supported the student's application for his job and had also taught the student's older brother in a previous class. The teacher had worked with the student to begin the process of gaining citizenship, a goal that the student had stated was very important to him. He was undocumented at the time he wrote this journal entry.

[Student] I'm sorry to be absent from class. My boss wanted me to work nights last week. I couldn't say no.

[Teacher] Why couldn't you say no?

[Student] I need the job. My boss knows I don't have papers. What could I do?

[Teacher] I understand your dilemma. We need to see about your citizenship papers. I'm disappointed in your boss. He's taking an unfair advantage of you.

[Student] I know, but I need the money, and I know he can find someone else if I quit. The warehouse is dangerous. Last week someone got hurt. He got sent home and told not to come back. Now what can he do? He can't work and he's afraid to see a doctor.

[Teacher] What about the local clinic? Have you called them? The Department of Public Health may also be interested in your workplace. Then there's always OSHA [Occupational Safety and Health Administration]. We will get help for your friend.

As a result of this exchange, the teacher was able to arrange for someone from the public health department to visit the class and talk about resources available to the class that were free. The teacher also arranged for a lawyer from the public defender's office to talk about the students' legal rights on the job. The goal of the participatory classroom is to enable learners to gain some control over their social environment. Learning the language provides them with a powerful tool, but it is not an end in itself. Student journals are an excellent tool to engage in problem posing (Norton, 1998). If successful, this process of problem posing can eventually lead to a transformation the whole community of learners.

Implications for Practice

Journal writing has become a popular tool in teacher preparation programs and in the second-language classroom. Teacher educators can use journals to encourage reflection among novice educators as they learn more about the teaching-learning transaction. For teacher educators with access to Web-based interactive software, journals can be placed on the Internet, thereby enabling teachers to extend their own reflections on action beyond the boundaries of the classroom. Among practicing adult educators, journals can help to provide a mechanism for effective staff development, especially for classroom teachers who are physically isolated from each other. Reflective journals can turn the practicing classroom teacher into a teacher-researcher by encouraging action research projects that are classroom based. Journals can provide a vehicle for the practitioner to reflect on action, ask questions, and begin the process of finding answers to common everyday problems that can help other teachers as well.

For second-language learners, interpersonal journals, such as dialogue journals, can provide the opportunity to practice authentic language through the interactions of writer and reader. Pressure to be correct is reduced by stressing the goal of communication, not grammatical accuracy. Fluency can be gained more readily through the simple act of writing for personal communication on topics of meaning to the writer. Journal writing can also be a powerful political tool in the emancipatory or participatory classroom. Journals can provide learners with the opportunities to reflect on practice and its implications for social change and personal empowerment.

Certainly, we have not seen the end of changes in educational philosophies that will continue to affect how we approach the teaching of ESL, nor have we seen the end to the development of new theories of how adults learn ESL. But there does appear to be widespread agreement that improved practice can result from ongoing personal reflection on practice. Practicing adult educators can be encouraged to make reflection a regular part of their own professional development program. Second-language learners can be encouraged to reflect on their learning as they develop their language skills. In both cases, journal writing can provide the vehicle for reflection that leads to more effective practice.

References

Auerbach, E. R. *Making Meaning, Making Change.* Washington, D.C.: Center for Applied Linguistics and Delta Systems, 1992.

Brock, M. N., Wong, M.M.W., and Yu, B. "Collaborative Diary Keeping." In D. Freeman, with S. Cornwell (eds.), *New Ways in Teacher Education.* Alexandria, Va.: Teachers of English to Speakers of Other Language, 1993.

Carroll, M. "Journal Writing as a Learning and Research Tool in the Adult Classroom." *TESOL Journal,* 1994, 4, 19–22.

Crandall, J. "Professionalism and Professionalization of Adult ESL Literacy." *TESOL Quarterly,* 1993, 27, 497–515.

Dong, Y. R. "Collective Reflection: Using Peer Responses to Dialogue Journals in Teacher Education." *TESOL Journal,* 1997, 7, 26–31.

Gebhard, J. G., and Oprandy, R. *Language Teaching Awareness: A Guide to Exploring Beliefs and Practices.* Cambridge: Cambridge University Press, 1999.

Johnson, D. M., and Roen, D. H. (eds.). *Richness in Writing: Empowering ESL Students.* White Plains, N.Y.: Longman, 1989.

Leki, 1. *Understanding ESL Writers: A Guide for Teachers.* Portsmouth, N.H.: Boynton/Cook, 1992.

Norton, B. "Using Journals in Second Language Research and Teaching." In T. Smoke (ed.), *Adult ESL: Politics, Pedagogy, and Participation in Classroom and Community Programs.* Hillside, N.J.: Erlbaum, 1998.

Nunan, D. *Language Teaching Methodology: A Textbook for Teachers.* Upper Saddle River, N.J.: Prentice Hall, 1990.

Pennycook, A. "Intoduction: Critical Approaches to TESOL." *TESOL Quarterly,* 1999, 33, 329–348.

Peyton, J. K. (ed.). *Students and Teachers Writing Together: Perspectives on Journal Writing.* Alexandria, Va.: Teachers of English to Speakers of Other Language, 1990.

Peyton, J. K., and Reed, L. *Dialogue Journal Writing with Nonnative English Speakers: A Handbook for Teachers.* Alexandria, Va.: Teachers of English to Speakers of Other Language, 1990.

Quigley, B. A., and Kuhne, G. W. (eds.). *Creating Practical Knowledge Through Action Research: Posing Problems, Solving Problems, and Improving Daily Practice.* New Directions for Adult and Continuing Education, no. 73. San Francisco: Jossey-Bass, 1997.

Raimes, A. *Techniques in Teaching Writing.* New York: Oxford University Press, 1983.

Richards, J. C., and Lockhart, C. *Reflective Teaching in Second Language Classrooms.* Cambridge: Cambridge University Press, 1994.

Richards, J. C., and Rodgers, T. S. *Approaches and Methods in Language Teaching: A Description and Analysis.* Cambridge: Cambridge University Press, 1986.

Richard A. Orem is professor of adult continuing education and literacy education at Northern Illinois University, DeKalb, Illinois.

8

Journal writing can be used for teaching and research in higher education in both on-site and distance-education modes.

Journal Writing in Higher Education

Peter Jarvis

Issues of teaching and learning, long accepted as important within adult education, are rapidly becoming significant in higher education. Nevertheless, journal writing, often referred to as a learning diary, is a teaching and learning technique that has not received a great deal of attention in the literature of higher education, despite the fact that diary writing is an old and established practice. In fact, in a rather rapid survey of the current higher education literature, I found very few articles on the subject; among the exceptions are those by Morrison (1996), Bush (1999), and Jasper (1999). Naturally, I refer to these works, but a great deal of what I discuss here is drawn from my own professional experience.

Before I became an adult educator, I was a teacher educator. It was in the early 1970s, in an early phase of my academic career, that I began to introduce reflective writing on practice to my own students. It is something that I have encouraged in different ways, at different stages, since that time. Journal writing, however, is useful inasmuch as it "may help adults break habitual modes of thinking and change life direction through reflective withdrawal and re-entry" (Lukinsky, 1990, p. 212). Jasper (1999), however, does point out that some students who keep reflective learning journals have found this process threatening; consequently, the introduction of this teaching and learning technique, as Fenwick points out Chapter Four, should be undertaken with some sensitivity.

Journaling can be used more widely than as reflective practice; it can be a teaching, learning, and research instrument in the fields of higher education. My own concern with this form of practice was based on necessity, since as a teacher-educator, I was expected to supervise students' teaching practice in schools in the geographic catchment area of the college at which I taught. Academic staff were expected to observe students teach at least twice a week

New Directions for Adult and Continuing Education, no. 90, Summer 2001
© John Wiley & Sons, Inc.1

during their eight weeks of teaching practice in their final year, and each member of staff usually had about four students to supervise. However, staff were also teaching the students in the other years of the college program. This meant that while the students were teaching in schools, academic staff's visits were curtailed. In fact, I was able to observe only a maximum of about two lessons a week for each student, which provided very little basis on which to assist them with their teaching skills or to assess their ability to be a teacher.

The college expected the students to provide a lesson plan, setting out aims, objectives, content, methods, and evaluation, for each lesson that they taught. It was from these plans that I got the inspiration to ask students to write about their practice. I asked the students for long, detailed evaluations of their teaching sessions rather than the short, cursory evaluation notes that they frequently made. Students had traditionally placed the emphasis on their preparation rather than their reflections.

I explained to these student teachers that although I would observe them teach twice a week, I would not always have the time to read their lesson plans thoroughly before they taught. Rather, I would read them after the lesson, and I would place greater emphasis on their own extensive evaluation of each lesson they taught. In other words, their notes formed the foundations for supervisory tutorials. Instead of my writing a few lines of evaluation, I was asking the students to write pages of self-evaluation. I asked them to evaluate every part of their lesson in terms of their practice and the plans that they had prepared. I asked them to write about what was good as well as what was not so good, how they had handled difficult situations, why they deviated from their planned lesson, and so on. As students began to write more, their evaluations gradually got sharper, and the tutorials became lively affairs. In fact, long before the ideas of learning journals or even reflective practice became the vogue, these students were writing their own learning journals.

Because the School of Educational Studies at the University of Surrey, where I teach, has always had an initial training course for educators of adults, I continued to use reflective practice whenever I trained them. We worked with a variety of professional groups: traditional adult educators, nurse and midwifery educators, and even teachers of young adults.

Reflective practice found its way into the educational vocabulary with the publication of Schön's *Reflective Practitioner* (1983), a book that has changed the way many people think about their practice and has led to many innovations in teaching and research. At the same time, my own very early experience with long evaluative reports written by the students about their own practice was the time in my own academic career when I began to question the traditional relationship between practice and theory. This eventually lead to my writing *The Practitioner Researcher* (Jarvis, 1999), in which I tried to work out something more about this relationship—but this happened only after I had begun to get students to use learning journals in their own doctoral research.

Journals in Undergraduate and Postgraduate Education

Morrison (1996) notes that since 1990, the University of Durham has required students to keep their own learning journal throughout the whole of their academic program at the university, although his own research was conducted with higher degree students. Indeed at Durham, the learning journal must be used as part of a compulsory assignment, requiring students to draw on data from the journal and reflect on them in terms of their own actions and their personal and professional development, although the contents are always confidential to individual student. The journal serves two reflective purposes. First, it helps students to become reflective learners, recording data about reading, study habits, and attitudes. Students are also invited to write about their own personal development; that is, they can record information about their increasing knowledge and their increasing ability to identify and articulate issues, and they can reflect on important decisions that they have taken since they enrolled in the program. Second, students can examine their own self-development and their own feelings of empowerment. In this regard, Morrison (1996) cites the work of Prawat (1991) to demonstrate this fact. Morrison notes that when reflective practice prospers, "it is seen as by many students as a major significant feature of their development in all spheres" (p. 328).

Bush (1999) records that he kept a journal while teaching adult student nurses about "spirituality and spiritual care in nursing practice" (p. 20). His entries, which were made within six hours of teaching and reexamined within two days, illustrate how he was grappling with both the teaching of the subject and the mature learners whom he was teaching. He recorded his thoughts about the teaching and the participation of students in this rather emotive but significant topic and concluded, "The keeping of a journal provided the educator with an opportunity to connect thoughts, feeling and action and relate them to what was happening now, as opposed to writing about what has already happened. . . . It encouraged the author to trace the development of any emerging interest and provided a personal account of any growth with a factual reference, that was repeatedly examined in order to create some personal meaning" (p. 26). As a result of his experiences, Bush (1999) has decided that in future courses, he will also ask students to keep their own journals about the program.

Jasper (1999), in a research project on the use of journaling that used grounded theory, discovered that all the students who used journaling thought that they had changed and developed as a result. However, she also discovered that one could not assume that students knew how to write a reflective journal; these skills had to be taught. Once the students had acquired the skills, however, journal writing could be used as a learning strategy, and it became an instrument for both personal and professional growth.

The Personal Use of Journals in Postgraduate Distance Teaching

I have been involved with learning journals in distance and mixed-mode delivery professional education. The first use is based on the idea of reflective teaching and learning through the medium of traditional distance education, and the second is about relating practice and theory in mixed-mode delivery, professional, continuing education.[1]

One of the traditional criticisms of distance education is that there is a tendency for the delivery of the teaching materials to be didactic, and much of it is. However, it is possible through the use of journals to make the course reflective and almost interactive. The department in which I work at the University of Surrey introduced distance-learning master's degree programs internationally in the early 1980s. They followed what has now become a rather traditional format of textbooks, study guides, and assignments, but more recently in my own courses, I have introduced the learning journal. I have used the learning journal in two different ways: to help students see how their own ideas are changing and developing as the course proceeds and to test their practice against the theoretical ideas to which they have been introduced.

Both the prescribed textbooks and the associated study guides are provided by the School of Educational Studies, although learners are encouraged to read more widely. At the beginning of the course, I suggest to the students that they start a learning diary, and I inform them that they will be given exercises and activities that can be usefully undertaken in such a learning journal. Two examples will suffice here. First, in a module on theories of learning, students are asked at the start of the course to record in their learning diary their own definition of learning; they are informed that they will refer to this definition frequently. As the students examine different theories and theorists, they are asked at different stages to write down their current definition of learning or to revisit their original definition and revise it in the light of their current understanding. In this way, students can trace their own learning through the program, becoming critically aware of their initial assumptions and developing other insights.

Second, since the department has students from around the world, we try not to be culturally imperialistic and expect learners from other cultures to accept Western scholarship unless it is valid in their own situation. Consequently, students are told that they should not accept uncritically what they read; when we give them activities or ask them questions about the Western theories they are studying, they should be critical and try things out in their own practice. If they work, then they might discuss in their learning diaries why they are valid. If the ideas do not work, their practice is not necessarily wrong, but they might want to consider the reasons that the Western theories seem inappropriate for their own practice. In this second exercise, the relationship between theory and practice is problematized because there is no assumption that a Western theory has any validity for non-Western societies. Naturally, this view brings into question the traditional Western assumption, prevalent since the Enlightenment, of a universality of knowledge. It also acknowledges Foucault's idea of the power of the dominant discourse (Sheridan, 1980) of Western theoretical approaches.

In both examples, the journal is a reflective learning tool based in the cognitive domain. However, in a recent professional continuing-education course, for a master's degree for management consultants, the learning journal was used in a different manner. This course has a mixed-mode delivery in which there is a set textbook, but the study guides are written for each module of work rather than based on the textbook. In this situation, the practice becomes the foundation for study, because the study guides are written by practitioners, although they contain a great deal of theory. In addition, the learners are professional practitioners who have had considerable professional experience and are taking this course in their spare time while they work. They were asked to base many of their reflections on their practice. This example of work-based learning uses journals as one means of learning in practice. However, practice is not merely cognitive; therefore, the learners are asked to include attitudinal and emotive dimensions in their reflection. The journal helps practitioners to focus on the wider aspects of their practice, such as emotional intelligence (Goleman, 1998), beliefs, and attitudes. Because this was a mixed-mode delivery course, the learners had occasional face-to-face study days in which they were asked to bring their journals and raise issues that had occurred in their practice and their studies. Their journals, however, remained entirely private; they were not seen by academic staff or fellow students unless the writers privileged others with access.

The Use of Journals in Research

As qualitative research is gaining acceptance in research in the education of adults, the use of the journal in the research process is becoming more widely recognized. For instance, in all forms of anthropological studies, researchers have always had to keep field notes (see Tandon, 1981, as an example of how the journal might be used), and I have had educational students conducting doctoral research in different societies and with people of different cultures. Their field notes form the record of their research findings. Moreover, action research (Carr and Kemmis, 1986), participative research (see Eldon, 1981, as an example), and practitioner research (Jarvis, 1999) are approaches within the qualitative domain of research that doctoral students increasingly are using. Their own record of the events becomes part of their research data. Practitioner researchers are frequently using their own practice as a research site, and their own involvement is part of the research process. In recent years, I have had doctoral students using journals in a variety of research situations.

A nurse educator who worked with me tried to understand how the subject of care might be taught to nursing and midwifery students. As part of her research, she spent twenty days as an observer in different types of care situations. She also was encouraged to keep a journal of her observations and reflections on the caring processes during this period. Her notes became the basis for the subsequent interviews that she conducted with the carers, so that she could ask quite incisive questions about specific care situations. In this way, she was able to probe the carers' understanding and reasons for what they were doing. She kept notes of the interviews as well, and by synthesizing her journal and the notes that she took during her interviews, she was able to understand more about the carers' own understanding of the relationship between practice and theory, more about reflective practice itself, and begin to understand how care can be learned, if not taught, in a formal mode. The journal became a significant part of her research data in the final presentation of her thesis. (In Chapter Five, Gillis gives other examples of how the nursing profession is using learning journals.)

Keeping a journal also became very important in a piece of action research relating to the teaching of art to adults that another doctoral student undertook. Many adults come to art classes to learn to draw and paint through copying already produced works of art rather than learning to become creative artists themselves. Trying to get them to change their approach to art is a difficult process, especially since these classes have to be financially self-supporting. Losing dissatisfied students can put the classes' viability at risk. But merely teaching students to reproduce other people's art can be less than satisfying for art teachers; consequently, some give up teaching. A doctoral student, who was also the head of an art department, kept a journal about the way that a creative art degree was introduced and the cognitive and emotive reactions of the students and his own staff involved in the process. A full learning diary was kept, both of his own experiences and those of his students and staff that he was able to ascertain over the period of many months. These entries became data on which interviews with staff were conducted and also the issues on which a focus group of art teachers concentrated. This approach highlighted many problems that are prevalent in adult education in the United Kingdom at this time, but since this in-depth piece of research focused on one college, he was only able to frame hypotheses about teaching adults art in the wider society.

The final piece of research to which I want to refer here is another doctoral study. Seeking to understand more fully all the aspects of the role of human resource development personnel, another of my doctoral students kept a journal of everything she did and everything people said to her about human resource development in the performance of her professional role. This study entailed far more than merely arranging training courses. The journal highlighted the amount of time she spent performing roles as diverse as needs analyst, strategist, administrator, consultant, counselor, and even spokesperson for management. Her journal not only helped her to understand more fully her role in her own doctoral research, but it became the basis of a handbook on human resource development that she and I subsequently wrote (Hargreaves and Jarvis, 2000).

In all of the research that I have described, the phenomenon under investigation is not some object lying outside the being of the researcher; rather, it is about making meaning of lived experience that cannot be replicated. The researchers are either recording and making meaning of their own experiences or interpreting the experiences of others. In all of these cases, the researcher is an interpreter and the reflective journal a means for recording and analyzing data; it is both research and lived experience (Van Manen, 1990).

Conclusion

Although this chapter contains a great deal that is autobiographical, it nevertheless reflects the practices of others with whom I have discussed the education of adults, and it is also in line with the literature on the subject.

In higher education in the United Kingdom, there is an increasing emphasis on record keeping, especially records of students' progress. Although the purpose is often portrayed as managerial, there is another sense in which such records might form the basis for some academic staff to keep their own journals. However, the fact that this approach is perceived by many to be a managerial exercise and a paper chase might inhibit the development of reflective journal writing among faculty.

Writing full, reflective journals is a time-consuming process, and the lack of extra time of many academics might also inhibit this development. There is little record in the literature regarding the amount of time that needs to be invested in this process, but I recall from my earliest experiences that students lacked the time to write the full evaluations for which I was asking. It is significant that Jasper (1999) does not mention time as an important issue in writing reflective journals, although this was not the focus of her research.

Nevertheless, keeping a journal is not only a useful learning exercise; it is essential to some forms of research. Keeping journals illustrates that the relationship between practice and theory is problematic and encourages critical reflection in different approaches to teaching and learning. Using reflective journals might be even more useful in lifelong learning as data are now being downloaded from the Web in greater amounts, without any guidance as to their validity.

Above all, writing learning diaries is an invaluable tool that can lead to personal and professional enrichment and empowerment. It should be practiced and taught much more widely in higher and continuing education.

Note

1. This approach to learning practice reflects ideas that have been developed by the Human Potential Development Group in the School of Educational Studies, a member of which I worked with in the development of this course.

References

Bush, T. "Journalling and the Teaching of Spirituality." *Nurse Education Today,* 1999, *19,* 20–28.

Carr, W., and Kemmis, S. *Becoming Critical: Education, Knowledge and Action Research.* Bristol, Pa.: Falmer Press, 1986.

Eldon, M. "Sharing the Research Work: Participative Research and Its Role Demands." In P. Reason and J. Rowan (eds.), *Human Inquiry.* New York: Wiley, 1981.

Goleman, D. *Working with Emotional Intelligence.* New York: Bantam Books, 1998.

Hargreaves, P., and Jarvis, P. *The Human Resource Development Handbook.* (Rev. ed.) London: Kogan Page, 2000.

Jarvis, P. *The Practitioner Researcher.* San Francisco: Jossey-Bass, 1999.

Jasper, M. "Nurses' Perceptions of the Value of Written Reflection." *Nurse Education Today,* 1999, *19,* 452–463.

Lukinsky, J. "Reflective Withdrawal Through Journal Writing." In J. Mezirow and others (eds.), *Fostering Critical Reflection in Adulthood.* San Francisco: Jossey-Bass, 1990.

Morrison, K. "Developing Reflective Practice in Higher Degree Students Through a Learning Journal." *Studies in Higher Education,* 1996, *31,* 317–332.

Prawat, R. S. "Conversations with Self and Conversations with Settings: A Framework for Thinking About Teacher Empowerment." *American Educational Research Journal,* 1991, *28,* 737–757.

Schön, D. *The Reflective Practitioner.* New York: Basic Books, 1983.

Sheridan, A. *Michael Foucault: The Will to Truth.* London: Tavistock, 1980.

Tandon, R. "Dialogue as Inquiry and Intervention." In P. Reason and J. Rowan (eds.), *Human Inquiry.* New York: Wiley, 1981.

Van Manen, M. *Researching Lived Experience.* Albany, N.Y.: SUNY Press, 1990.

Peter Jarvis is professor of continuing education, University of Surrey, England.

9

This chapter highlights the themes from the previous chapters, identifies the challenges of implementing journal writing, and offers suggestions for further reading.

Journal Writing in Practice: From Vision to Reality

Leona M. English, Marie A. Gillen

The word *journal* has its roots in the French word *jour* (day). The corresponding word *journey* came to refer to the amount of traveling that a person could do in a day. In turn, the word *journal* has come to mean daily writing about one's journey (Schiwy, 1996). A journal provides a place where a learner or an educator can record what is happening in class, everyday life, or a professional relationship, whether daily or weekly or monthly. This book has been about that type of writing, that is, writing focused on learning from daily experience. Just as well-known journal writers like Anne Frank (1967), Etty Hillesum (1985), and Anaïs Nin (1966) have used the journal forum to write about their lives, we encourage adult education practitioners and researchers to begin and continue to come to knowing through journal writing.

Chapter Themes

Writing can be an intimidating and challenging experience for even the most seasoned of writers. Cixous (1989) captures this fear when she poses the question, "And why don't you write?" and then answers: "Writing is for you, you are for you. . . . I know why you haven't written. . . . Because writing is at once too high, too great for you, it's reserved for the great" (p. 574). The challenge for adult educators is to encourage the writing process as a positive learning and language practice. Our vision of how this language practice can be enacted has been brought to life vividly by the authors of each of the chapters in this book. We concur with David Boud, who, in Chapter One, describes journal writing as a reflective practice that allows

NEW DIRECTIONS FOR ADULT AND CONTINUING EDUCATION, no. 90, Summer 2001
© John Wiley & Sons, Inc.

for "puzzling through what is happening in our work and in our lives." Such puzzling is a way of learning how to make sense of experience. Similarly, Roger Hiemstra, in Chapter Two, identifies journal writing as a record of earlier reflections that can be reviewed and reread, therefore making a "progressive clarification of insights possible." He sees journal writing as an "investment in yourself through a growing awareness of personal thoughts and feelings." The authors of the chapters unanimously view journals as a means of knowing.

Although Leona M. English, in Chapter Three, accepts and appreciates journal writing as a positive teaching and learning practice, she asks critical questions about how ethics intersects with journal writing. These questions highlight the need for ethical guidelines such as maintaining a balance between the personal and the professional and respecting the integrity of the practice, as well as the relationship between the narrator and the reader. In Chapter Four, Tara J. Fenwick focuses on the complex issue of responding adequately to journal entries, a task that often falls to adult educators. She presents her thoughts on how adult educators can respond to journal writing in ways that respect the writer, the responder, and the learning context. Fenwick discusses ideas on grading and addresses the issue of conflict in the educator-learner relationship.

In Chapter Five, Angela J. Gillis considers how journal writing can be used in the education of health professionals such as nurses and community nutrition educators and in community programs. Gillis explains how the use of journal writing provides a holistic approach to health education that includes personal, emotional, cognitive, and spiritual dimensions. In Chapter Six, Elizabeth A. Peterson and Ann Jones explore the use of journal writing in the education of women. They profile the benefits, challenges, and potential of journal writing for increasing women's social awareness, personal growth, and critical reflection. They point out how journal writing challenges women to reflect and focus in greater depth on their own subjective knowledge and how journal writing increases women's learning in a variety of settings such as continuing professional education and higher education.

In Chapter Seven, Richard A. Orem examines how journal writing has been used to enhance the teaching of English as a Second Language (ESL). Using selections from his own teaching journal and selections from his students, Orem argues that journal writing can shape the learning experience and contribute to the professional development of ESL teachers and the knowledge base of learners. In Chapter Eight, Peter Jarvis situates journal writing in the pedagogical practices of higher education. He develops through the use of many examples the idea that journals can assist in the processes of student research and data collection, as well as in the humanizing of distance education. He encourages students to engage in journal writing as a narrative process that leads to personal and professional learning.

Our goal in bringing together the writers for this volume was to claim a central place for journal writing within the field of adult education. We believe that we have achieved this goal, and we concur with Cixous (1989) that writing is for everyone; it is not a practice reserved for English literature specialists. As we see it, journal writing is an important part of the teaching and learning process; it is central to the reflective practice approach of adult education and a good way of keeping track of the development of ideas and of monitoring works in progress. As far as we are aware, there is no other volume in the adult education literature that focuses specifically on the use of journal writing in adult education.

Remaining Questions and Missing Voices

Inspired by the critically reflective practice of Wilson and Hayes (2000) and consistent with the reflective practice orientation of this volume, we offer a critique of our own work and the volume in general. In part, we invite others into the conversation on journal writing and adult education, and in part we identify our own uncertainty and lack of clarity on some of the issues that journal writing raises.

A review of the chapters has left us with some questions. First, if journal writing is integral to the process of enhancing reflective practice and is an effective means for doing so, as David Boud suggests, why is so little empirical research available on journal writing? Although areas such as mathematics education (Jurdak and Zein, 1998) have yielded significant data on the effectiveness of journal writing to improve teaching and learning, few empirical studies exist on this topic in adult education. Notable among the existing studies is that of Holt (1994), who invites researchers and practitioners to do follow-up work on the effectiveness of journals. Could it be that adult educators are not interested in the topic or take its use for granted? Certainly, all those who contributed to this volume have used journal writing in their classes, yet none of them offers data, beyond those collected anecdotally, to support the use of journal writing. In addition, the fact that the largely theoretically based *Handbook of Adult and Continuing Education* (Wilson and Hayes, 2000) contains no index citations for journal writing or even for writing in general concerns us greatly. The challenge to study the educational value of journal writing further beckons us.

Second, how does one resolve the unreconciled tension created by the gaps or missing voices in this volume? In the light of our earlier work (English and Gillen, 2000b), the most obvious gap in this volume is a thorough discussion of the connections among and between topics like spirituality, adult learning, and journal writing. Although Hiemstra's chapter addresses spirituality generally, the intersection of journal writing, spirituality, and adult learning cries out for further exploration. We are mindful of the strong tradition of journal writing in spirituality that is represented well by writers such as Progoff (1975), who explored the use of the intensive journal method as a vehicle for those on a spiritual journey, and Augustine (1949), who used his journal, *Confessions,* to nourish Western spirituality more deeply. Although some writers in adult education, like Zeph (2000), English and Gillen (2000a), and Vogel (2000), have pointed out the value of using journal writing in a learning context as a way to foster spirituality, they too have stopped short of an extensive exploration, along this line of inquiry, specifically for adult education.

Another gap that is not addressed in this volume is the use of the cyberjournal, or the exchange of information back and forth through e-mail. The use of a cyberjournal (English and Lander, 2000) or the use of e-mail as a dialogic learning journal allows the participants (often faculty member and students) to track their responses to each other by co-creating another text to reflect on. We see untold possibilities in the use of the cyberjournal as a way for the narrators to activate and sustain their critical capacities and engage in a process of continuous meaning making.

Finally, the authors of this volume have responded well to our editorial call to use a framework of reflective practice as they developed their ideas on journal writing. Reflective practice, as described by David Boud in Chapter One, is "a device for working with events and experience to extract meaning from them." We acknowledge, however, that this "reflection is not, in and of itself, necessarily critical" (Brookfield, 2000, p. 37). With the exception of Fenwick and English's chapters, there is little exploration of the use of journals from the perspective of critically reflective practice, the intent of which is to bring ideological critique to bear on the issue, especially as it relates to the power dimensions of learning.

We invite our colleagues in adult education to take up these challenges, to build on this introductory volume, and to flesh out the various connections between journal writing and adult education that have been presented in this volume. We welcome the dialogue.

The Challenge of the Writing Process

Although journal writing holds the promise of helping us find "meaning in the world by exploring it through language" (Fulwiler, 1987, p. 1), we acknowledge that writing is just plain hard work, even for those who identify with the title writer. By writing in the first person—claiming personal authority in our writing and processing of ideas—we advocate trying to find meaning in our own written word.

Our position on writing is perhaps best illustrated by an example. Leona once had a drama teacher, a no-nonsense character, who ran her classes like clockwork and demanded hard work and professionalism of her students and of herself. On the first day of the second term, a very intense and self–conscious woman entered the room and joined the vocalization class. The drama teacher asked each participant to recite the nursery rhyme story of Jack and Jill from a different perspective (for example, newspaper reporter, tabloid writer, newscaster, local gossip). The new student spent about ten minutes thinking about her part and trying to get into the mind of the character. The drama teacher, who grew impatient with this delay, said, "Acting's a job; get on with it!" And we did. The new student was shocked. Similarly, writing is a job to get on with. Although we recognize the value of muses, good ideas most often come to prepared minds, not ones waiting for divine inspiration. Journal writing is for all of us, whether we call ourselves writers or not.

Language Features of Writing a Journal

What does a good journal entry look like? How can you learn to be comfortable with journal writing? We borrow the following specific suggestions about journal writing from Fulwiler (1987):

- Write in colloquial diction—journal entries do not have to be fancy or formal. In fact, they can be written in everyday language, using abbreviations and contractions. These shortcuts give you, the writer, freedom.
- Write in the first person. The use of the first person as narrator is one way of ensuring that the journal entry is about you and what you think, or have come to know.
- Use informal punctuation in your writing. Again, the journal entry need not be formal—it ought to be focused primarily on putting your thoughts on paper.
- Write using the rhythms of everyday speech. When you use everyday idioms you can more easily have a conversation going that invites you and others into a dialogue.
- Experiment with your writing. As the journal writer, you need to be able to write what you want without fear of reprisal or correction.

Journals have special language features that are often informal rather than formal. A conversational style of journal writing is a helpful way to start writing a journal. Overcoming our fears of writing in less than perfect English is one of the biggest fears of beginning writers. In fact, even experienced writers probably suffer fear from time to time.

Suggestions for Further Reading

Readers of this volume may want to move more deeply into the writing process, to know more about what is written on journal writing, and to identify gaps in the research literature. To respond to this need, we suggest some reading on journal writing that we have found particularly helpful. None of these is specifically on journal writing in adult education, since no such resource exists.

Baldwin, C. *Life's Companion: Journal Writing as a Spiritual Quest*. New York: Bantam, 1991.

This helpful and carefully written book for people who never have written in a personal journal links journal writing with inner development and self-knowledge. The strength of the book is its inclusion of wonderful quotations regarding journal writing, challenging journal writing exercises for the beginner and the more mature writer, and questions to help writers begin the journal writing process. Baldwin attends to dreams, the body, intuition, and ritual as part of journal writing; she sees it as a way to enhance spiritual development. She also includes a variety of formats and examples such as freewriting, timed writing, and unsent letters. This is a book written primarily for those who are using journals for personal growth.

Cameron, J. *The Artist's Way: A Spiritual Path to Higher Creativity*. Los Angeles: Tarcher, 1992.

This book details a journal writing process that Cameron has named "the morning pages." This process requires writing three pages, with a pen and paper, without too much thinking, on arising in the morning; this exercise is basically a "stream of consciousness" (p. 10). The morning pages technique is an established way of beginning journal writing, because it makes the novice writer suspend all judgment about what is being written. The morning pages is a way of clearing whatever is on the writer's mind or in the writer's heart. It ultimately is a way of enhancing or fostering creativity. It forces writing, even if the results are not always lucid or meaningful. Cameron's book provides other useful ideas, encouraging writers to write and be creative.

Fulwiler, T. (ed.). *The Journal Book*. Portsmouth, N.H.: Boynton/Cook, 1987.

This is a collection of essays on journal writing in a number of educational venues and disciplines, including English, arts and humanities, and the quantitative disciplines. It is one of the few books that focuses on journal writing in educational or learning contexts, as opposed to journal writing for personal development. *The Journal Book* contains forty-two chapters written by a variety of writers, including language scholars such as Peter Elbow and Ann Berthoff, as well as subject specialists in each of the disciplines named. This is not a how-to book; the first of the three sections, for instance, presents the theoretical issues relating to the language of speculation. Peter Elbow and Jennifer Clarke's chapter in this section, "Desert Island Discourse: The Benefits of Ignoring Audience," provides an interesting exploration of how writers' awareness of an audience affects their voice. The various chapter authors foreground the importance of exploring the world through language. They claim that humans learn through language and, more especially, that "when people write about something they learn it better" (Fulwiler, 2000, p. 9).

Moon, J. *Learning Journals: A Handbook for Academics, Students and Professional Development*. London: Kogan Page, 1999.
This book provides a creative synthesis of information on using journal writing for reflective learning. The author, who has written previous books on reflection in learning, focuses on how to use journal writing as part of the educational process as a way to enhance reflection. Moon explores how to create the conditions that are necessary for reflection. She also examines the role of journals in promoting learning for academic, personal, and professional learning. The most helpful feature of the book is its extensive and current bibliography on journal writing, which will be of considerable use to both neophytes and experienced journal writers.

Progoff, I. *At a Journal Workshop: The Basic Text and Guide for Using the Intensive Journal Process*. New York: Dialogue House Library, 1975.
Progoff is one of the most significant figures in the literature on journal writing; indeed, his name has become synonymous with the journal writing process. He studied with Carl Jung and consequently was deeply influenced by Jung's understanding of the power of the unconscious. The objective of Progoff's method, the intensive journal method (IJM), is to get people in touch with their deepest questions, desires, creative potential, and spiritual needs. According to the IJM, the writer engages in dialogue with the persons, works, body, and events in his or her life. Although the IJM can be done on one's own, the method is often taught in workshops by individuals who are certified in the Progoff journal process.

Schiwy, M. A. *A Voice of Her Own: Women and the Journal-Writing Journey*. New York: Fireside, 1996.
This book includes many excerpts from journals from such illustrious writers as Carolyn Heilbrun, Anaïs Nin, and May Sarton. According to Schiwy, journals help women to understand themselves, to grow, to become more reflective, and to make sense of their lives in ways that cannot be said aloud. Schiwy provides practical examples that can help the reader begin and continue a helpful learning process. She reviews many aspects of keeping a journal, such as how keeping a journal can give meaning to one's life, and she provides an overview of different types and varieties of journals. She profiles the history of why women keep journals and diaries (she equates the two formats) and believes that journals, because of their personal content and inclusion of feelings as well as thoughts, are particularly well suited for women's learning.

References

Augustine. *The Confessions of Saint Augustine*. New York: Modern Library, 1949.
Brookfield, S. D. "The Concept of Critically Reflective Practice." In A. L. Wilson and E. R. Hayes (eds.), *Handbook of Adult and Continuing Education*. San Francisco: Jossey-Bass, 2000.

Cixous, H. "The Laugh of the Medusa." In S. D. Ross (ed.), *Art and Its Significance*. New York: SUNY Press, 1989.

English, L. M., and Gillen, M. A. "A Postmodern Approach to Adult Religious Education." In A. L. Wilson and E. R. Hayes (eds.), *Handbook of Adult and Continuing Education*. San Francisco: Jossey-Bass, 2000a.

English, L. M., and Gillen, M. A. (eds.). *Addressing the Spiritual Dimensions of Adult Learning*. New Directions for Adult and Continuing Education, no. 85. San Francisco: Jossey-Bass, 2000b.

English, L. M., and Lander, D. "Increasing Reflection and Dialogue in Distance Learning." *Journal for the Art of Teaching*, 2000, 7, 85–95.

Frank, A. *Anne Frank: The Diary of a Young Girl*. New York: Washington Square Press, 1967.

Fulwiler, T. (ed.). *The Journal Book*. Portsmouth, N.H.: Boynton/Cook, 1987.

Hillesum, E. *An Interrupted Life: The Diaries of Etty Hillesum, 1941–43*. New York: Washington Square Press, 1985.

Holt, S. "Reflective Journal Writing and Its Effects on Adults." In *The Year in Review*, Vol. 3: *1993–1994*. Dayton, Va.: Virginia Adult Educators Research Network, 1994. (ED 375 302)

Jurdak, M., and Zein, R. A. "The Effect of Journal Writing on Achievement in and Attitudes Toward Mathematics." *School Science and Mathematics*, 1998, 98, 412–419.

Nin, A. *The Diary of Anais Nin*, Vol. 1: *1931–1934*. (G. Stuhlmann, ed.). New York: Harcourt Brace Jovanovich, 1966.

Progoff, I. *At a Journal Workshop: The Basic Text and Guide for Using the Intensive Journal Process*. New York: Dialogue House Library, 1975.

Schiwy, M. A. *A Voice of Her Own: Women and the Journal Writing Journey*. New York: Fireside, 1996.

Vogel, L. J. "Reckoning with the Spiritual Lives of Adult Educators." In L. M. English and M. A. Gillen (eds.), *Addressing the Spiritual Dimensions of Adult Learning*. New Directions for Adult and Continuing Education, no. 85. San Francisco: Jossey-Bass, 2000.

Wilson, A. L., and Hayes, E. R. (eds.). *Handbook of Adult and Continuing Education*. San Francisco: Jossey-Bass, 2000.

Zeph, C. P. "The Spiritual Dimensions of Lay Ministry Programs." In L. M. English and M. A. Gillen (eds.), *Addressing the Spiritual Dimensions of Adult Learning*. New Directions for Adult and Continuing Education, no. 85. San Francisco: Jossey-Bass, 2000.\

Leona M. English is associate professor of adult education at Saint Francis Xavier University, Antigonish, Nova Scotia.

Marie A. Gillen is professor of adult education at Saint Francis Xavier University Antigonish, Nova Scotia.

INDEX

Back Issue/Subscription Order Form

Copy or detach and send to:

Jossey-Bass, 350 Sansome Street, San Francisco CA 94104-1342

Call or fax toll free!

Phone 888-378-2537 6AM-5PM PST; Fax 800-605-2665

Back issues: Please send me the following issues at $27 each.

(Important: please include series initials and issue number, such as ACE78.)

1. ACE _____

_____

_____

$ _____ Total for single issues

$ _____ Shipping charges (for single issues **only;** subscriptions are exempt from shipping charges): Up to $30, add $5^{50} • $30^{01}–$50, add $6^{50} $50^{01}–$75, add $8 • $75^{01}–$100, add $10 • $100^{01}–$150, add $12 Over $150, call for shipping charge.

Subscriptions Please ❑ start ❑ renew my subscription to *New Directions for Adult and Continuing Education* for the year _____ at the following rate:

U.S.:	❑ Individual $59	❑ Institutional $114
Canada/Mexico:	❑ Individual $59	❑ Institutional Canada $154
All Others:	❑ Individual $83	❑ Institutional $188

NOTE: Subscriptions are quarterly, and are for the calendar year only. . Subscriptions begin with the Spring issue of the year indicated above. Prices are subject to change.

$ _____ Total single issues and subscriptions (Add appropriate sales tax for your state for single issues. No sales tax on U.S. subscriptions. Canadian residents, add GST for subscriptions and single issues.)

❑ Payment enclosed (U.S. check or money order only)

❑ VISA, MC, AmEx, Discover Card #_____ Exp. date_____

Signature _____ Day phone _____

❑ Bill me (U.S. institutional orders only. Purchase order required.)

Purchase order #_____

Federal Tax I.D. 135593032   GST 89102-8052

Name _____

Address _____

_____

Phone_____ E-mail _____

For more information about Jossey-Bass, visit our Web site at:
www.josseybass.com   **PRIORITY CODE = ND1**

Jossey-Bass regrets that the index to *New Directions for Adult and Continuing Education* 90 was not up to our usual high standards. Because we strive to provide high-quality indexes for all our publications, we are providing a new index for that issue, which we hope you will find complete and easy to use.

INDEX

LaVergne, TN USA
09 September 2009
157240LV00004B/12/P

9 780787 957742